The Pilgrim's Inn Cookbook

TERRY FOSTER

The Pilgrim's Inn Cookbook

New recipes from
the coast of Maine

TERRY FOSTER

I wish to dedicate
this book to my parents,
Jack and Betty Foster

Illustrations by Michael Gellatly

© 1997 Pilgrim's Inn
P.O. Box 69
Deer Isle, Maine 04627

Cover photographs—
    Coastal scene: Terrell Lester
    Inn: Lynn Karlin
    Terry Foster: Sherry Streeter

Photography and book design by Sherry Streeter

ISBN 0-9659928-0-2

First Printing
Printed in the United States of America

ACKNOWLEDGMENTS

Writing this cookbook may never have happened if not for Jean and Dud's faith in me and in Pilgrim's Inn. They prevailed over my doubt with unfailing encouragement. Shrugging off my hesitation, they pushed me beyond my limits. I am thankful for their confidence, generosity, and constant support.

Special thanks to Joan Schlosstein for her patience, friendship, and valuable sweet tooth.

My gratitude to past and present kitchen staff members: Elaine Webb, Julie Adams, Rebekah Raye Woisard, Vicki Hull, Todd Waite, Judith Bradshaw, Karen Davis, Haley Robbins, and Cheryl Knowlton.

Many thanks to Priscilla and Carl Woodward for their incredibly fresh farm products; to Pam Pace, our mushroom sleuth; to Jack Hamblen for his mussels and always pleasant island spirit; to Pearl Hardie for his succulent scallops; to Skip Greenlaw of Stonington Lobster Co-op for his high-quality and fresh seafood; to Claude Dupuy of Nova Foods for his exceptional cheeses; to Harald Smedal for his wonderful produce and divine charm; and to Lloyd and Marge Capen for their delicious fall apples.

Sincere thanks to our customers, whose appetites contributed greatly to the development of the Pilgrim's Inn menu, and to my wife, Linda, for her love and assistance throughout my many hours in the kitchen and before the computer.

Lastly, I am very appreciative of Sherry Streeter, who generously worked with us with much enthusiasm and patience.

CONTENTS

FROM THE CHEF

Food is an altogether wonderful way of stimulating people and heightening their senses. I consider eating and cooking truly fresh food to be one of the pure pleasures of life. Food is festive. Endless varieties of flavors, scents, textures, and presentations capture the attention of those dining and heighten the convivial atmosphere at the table. My approach to cooking has always been one of unabashed enthusiasm. I am most content in the kitchen organizing and preparing a meal. There is a sense of accomplishment and gratification that comes from creating a dish and inspiring expressions of pleasure from those at the table. Unfortunately, we live in a society that favors fast artificial food and that seems detached from any real connection with the food it consumes. I feel very fortunate to know food at its absolute best—the pure sweetness of corn just picked and cooked, the rich color and fragrance of vine-ripened tomatoes, the cool-refreshing bite of baby arugula, and the wonderful scent of fresh herbs.

The fundamentals of our cooking at the Inn are simple: find which foods are at their peak, develop our own local resources, balance and harmonize flavors, shapes, colors, and textures, and fashion recipes and ideas to our own conditions. We cook what we like to eat and I suggest the same to anyone who cooks—there is considerable comfort and enjoyment in preparing food you like. We tend not to give much attention to food trends but to look to our own backyard gardens for menu ideas. There is no better purveyor of fine food than the garden. Freshness and availability are our first considerations when planning our nightly menus and our use of food only at its best contributes greatly to our success. Our idea of "freshness" is nasturtium flowers carefully picked moments before dinner to be lightly tossed with the salad. This commitment has also led us to the docks of nearby Stonington for the best seafood, to the woods for wild mushrooms, and to friends and neighbors for eggs, apples, rhubarb, and fresh berries. Changing our menu daily allows us the luxury of being able to serve food at its peak. Most people are unaccustomed to this, and to hear them say they "didn't believe food could be that good" is what our cooking is all about.

The recipes in this book present techniques and provide general guidance. They are not rigid and do not have to be followed exactly to guarantee success. My intent with these recipes is to emphasize the flavor of a dish by balancing and harmonizing ingredients. Adapt these recipes to your own personal tastes, resources, dietary restrictions, and ability. Season a dish with herbs and spices you like and notice how they affect the flavor. Make substitutions with seasonal ingredients from your region. A cook must put intuition and a sense of adventure into play when cooking. Part of the fun of cooking is using your imagination and being creative. Don't be intimidated, be flexible, and most of all trust your senses. Observe, feel, taste, and smell the ingredients and notice what happens to them in the cooking process. Knowing how fresh ingredients work together and treating them with respect can make the difference between an average dish and a sensational one. Attention to detail is an ingredient everyone can savor.

The perfect evening at the Inn is one that brings people together with good food, fine wine, a festive ambiance, and a sense of friendship. With these recipes I hope to share this experience and provide a foundation of guidelines that will further enhance your own style of cooking.   —*Terry Foster*

FROM THE INNKEEPERS

Lovestruck at 40, Jean and I set a course for Maine that fulfilled her life-long desire to live in the region and mine for less population pressure. Jean left her job as a high school counselor and owner of a fledgling restaurant in Annapolis, Maryland, and I abandoned a coaching career at New Hampshire's Dartmouth College. We had learned of an opportunity to lease, with an option to purchase, an inn—Pilgrim's Inn. The arrangement seemed like a fail-safe opportunity to assess our appetite for a project we could work on together and our ability to succeed where many like-minded dreamers have failed.

We began our first day (having arrived the night before) loaded down with supplies. Jean, an experienced and successful caterer, armed herself with a stack of recipes from her restaurant and the latest food magazines, readying herself for the formidable task of preparing dinner six days a week for an average of 20 guests a night. That first year, we had only one night with an empty dining room!

Jean had two assistants, employees we inherited from the previous owners: Linda McLaughlin, Mother Earth herself, and Rebekah Raye, a superb, free-spirited, and artistic baker. Linda and Bek provided much moral support and became our closest friends. Without them, we could never have survived our beginning years as innkeepers.

While Jean was caught up with kitchen duties, I undertook most of the hosting and bartending responsibilities. This proved challenging for one whose interest in alcoholic beverages barely goes beyond an occasional beer and for whom one cocktail party a year is adequate. We both took reservations, greeted guests, and cooked breakfast. Since we had no time to experience recreational options on Deer Isle ourselves, we planned guests' days by drawing on information provided by helpful employees and previous guests. In addition to Linda and Bek, we were blessed with Vicki Hull, Norma McGuffie, and Nancy Bogin. We all shared innkeeping responsibilities of housekeeping, bartending, taking reservations, and holding hands. Sixteen years later, they remain friends and employees.

Through the years, we have shared hard and good times and we have acquired a book's worth of retrospectively hilarious tales. Life at the Inn has become considerably easier as our staff has grown. Two major changes over the years have greatly enhanced our lives here: hiring Terry as chef in 1989 and renovating and moving into our own house nearby in 1992.

By 1989, we needed a change. Our innkeeping duties had left us with little time or energy for anything else. Insisting on using the best products and freshest ingredients to create meals that would be as pleasing to the eye as to the palate, Jean had attracted a large following. To our surprise, a letter arrived from someone in Maryland who shared a similar appreciation for fresh ingredients and creative cuisine, inquiring about a position as chef. Terry Foster had long dreamed of coming to Maine and the timing was perfect.

The three of us quickly learned that we shared more than commitment to fine dining. Our senses of humor and personalities meshed perfectly and we have become a real team. Terry and his staff have enabled us to spend more time in our gardens, which serve the Inn as well as our spirits.

Our 200-year-old inn has been redecorated, refurbished, and repainted many times in the last 15 years. Our reputation has grown, and we can proudly say we have hosted more than 18,000 guests. Though we have never articulated a formal business plan, our philosophy has not changed over the years. We approach each day with the same commitment to service—to provide our guests with personal attention and to ensure they have the best possible experience on our island. Pilgrim's Inn has allowed us to earn a living in a very special place. We live in a community in the truest sense, and we count among our close friends farmers, fishermen, artists, and retired executives "from away." We are delighted with this opportunity to share with you Terry's recipes and thoughts, to give you some glimpses of our inn, and to introduce you to some of the people who are responsible for our success.
                                                                —*Dud Hendrick*

Guests relaxing outside the Ark—now Pilgrim's Inn—in the early 1900s.

HISTORY OF PILGRIM'S INN

Today, Pilgrim's Inn, located at the head of Northwest Harbor on Deer Isle, plays an important role in the summer economy of Deer Isle Village. Guests visit from across the country and around the world and partake of what Deer Isle has to offer, visiting our artists and craftspeople and hiking and biking the island's trails and roads. The Inn, built in 1793 by Ignatius Haskell, has not always been a center of activity. The town, as well, has suffered bust and enjoyed boom. A glance at an abbreviated timeline provides insight into the evolution of the village. These snapshots enable us to picture what life may have been like in Northwest Harbor and at Pilgrim's Inn.

1500s–1600s — The Penobscot tribe of the Abenaki Indian nation arrived as Deer Isle's first summer people sometime in the early 1500s. In 1603, Martin Pring became the first Englishman to see Deer Isle, and Samuel de Champlain visited the area a year later.

1793 — Ignatius Haskell of Newburyport, Massachusetts, built his home at the head of the harbor. Along with his father, Mark, and brothers, he built a saw and grist mill at Northwest Harbor in 1772. Family history insists that Ignatius's wife refused to join him on Deer Isle until he built the grandest home there.

1800–1850s — Coastal trade dominated Deer Isle activity. The village boasted a millinery shop, a tannery, two stables, two sail lofts, a blacksmith shop, a cobbler shop, a customs office, and a post office. In 1806 the *Bolina*, Ignatius's first ship, was launched from his boatyard in Northwest Harbor.

1853–1900 — The arrival of the first steamship linked Deer Isle to the rest of the country. Lobsters, caught off Deer Isle and canned in island canneries, were shipped out of Northwest Harbor. Several Deer Isle men lost their lives in the Civil War. Late in the century, the first summer visitors began arriving. The village had three hotels, two of them year-round operations. The third was The Ark, which opened in 1890 and was run by Elizabeth Cush Haskell. It would later become Pilgrim's Inn.

1920–1940s — Deer Isle village continued as a commercial and social center for the northern half of the island. The village now comprised a grocery store, drug store, hardware store, printing shop, and gas plant. On summer evenings, residents from miles around walked to town to play pool (at one of two pool halls), see a movie, eat ice cream at the soda fountain, play basketball in the town hall at the mill dam, or roller-skate at the rink. At the end of each evening, lanterns flickered along the roads as folks made their way home. In 1938, the bridge to the mainland was built and coastal trade vanished. The granite quarrying nearly ceased and the population decreased. In 1944, Elizabeth Haskell died and The Ark was left unoccupied. The building fell into a state of neglect and disrepair.

1975 — Pilgrim's Inn, formerly The Ark, opened with George and Elli Pavloff as innkeepers. The former priest and potter were successful in placing the Inn in the National Register of Historic Places. Soon, Pilgrim's Inn was included in Norman Simpson's *Country Inns and Back Roads*, a very significant marketing coup in that era.

1982–Present — Jean and Dud Hendrick arrived from New Hampshire to lease Pilgrim's Inn. After the one-year lease expired, the Hendricks elected to exercise their option to buy. The Inn's reputation and popularity continue to grow with each passing year.

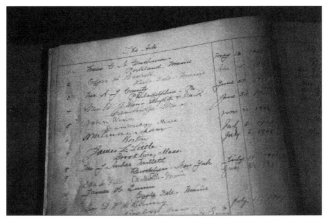

The Ark's guest register, 1901.

BREAKFASTS

LOBSTER, CHANTERELLE MUSHROOM, AND LEEK FRITTATA

Serves 6

Frittata are Italian omelets that combine many ingredients: vegetables, herbs, cheeses, seafood, and meats. They differ from American omelets, which are stuffed and folded over to form a half-moon shape. Frittata ingredients are incorporated into the eggs before cooking; when served, the frittata is left round and cut into wedges like a pie. In addition to breakfast, frittata can be sliced as a salad garnish or as a lunch entrée.

1 lobster (1½ pounds)
1 tablespoon unsalted butter
1 small leek, white part only, finely diced
4 ounces chanterelle mushrooms, finely diced
8 eggs

2 tablespoons heavy cream
2 tablespoons chopped fresh parsley
1 tablespoon chopped fresh chives
1 tablespoon chopped fresh chervil
Salt and pepper
2 tablespoons olive oil

1. Steam or boil the lobster for 10 minutes. Remove from heat and let stand until cool enough to handle. Crack the claws, knuckles, and tail section; remove the lobster meat and finely dice. Set aside.
2. Heat the butter in a small sauté pan over medium heat. Add the leek and mushrooms; sauté for 4 to 5 minutes, stirring occasionally. Set aside to cool.
3. Lightly beat the eggs with the cream in a large bowl. Stir in the lobster meat, mushroom mixture, and herbs; season with salt and pepper.
4. Heat the olive oil in a 10-inch nonstick skillet over medium heat; pour in the egg-lobster mixture. As the egg starts to cook, pierce the mixture and pull in the edges with a rubber spatula to allow the uncooked egg on top to move through to the bottom. When the frittata is almost set (firm but still somewhat liquid on top), place the pan under the broiler to finish cooking the top.
5. Slide the frittata onto a cutting board and cut into wedges. Serve hot or at room temperature.

TOMATO WELSH RAREBIT

Serves 6

This is a twist on the English classic. It makes a delicious breakfast served over warm Country Biscuits (page 6). It can be prepared ahead and refrigerated, then reheated over low heat until warm; but do not bring to a boil.

2 tablespoons unsalted butter
2 tablespoons all-purpose flour
1 teaspoon ground mustard
Pinch of cayenne pepper
1¼ cup milk

¼ cup heavy cream
2 cups grated Cheddar cheese
1 tomato, peeled, seeded, and
  chopped
Salt and pepper

1. Melt the butter in a saucepan over medium-low heat. Stir in the flour, mustard, and cayenne; cook for 2 to 3 minutes, stirring constantly.
2. Meanwhile, in another saucepan bring the milk and cream to a simmer over medium-high heat. Slowly whisk it into the butter-flour mixture. Bring to a boil, reduce the heat to low, and cook for 3 to 4 minutes, stirring occasionally.
3. Remove the mixture from the heat and stir in the cheese; whisk until smooth. Stir in the chopped tomato and season with salt and pepper. Serve hot.

SPINACH, WILD MUSHROOM, AND ARUGULA TART

Serves 8 to 10

This breakfast tart is good any time of the day. The spicy, peppery flavor of the arugula works well with the rich earthiness of the wild mushrooms. It is important to squeeze out as much liquid as possible from the cooked spinach so the tart won't be soggy. When selecting mushrooms, choose those that are fresh, dry, and firm—with no bruises or dark spots.

TART DOUGH
1/4 pound unsalted butter
2 tablespoons solid vegetable shortening
2 cups all-purpose flour
Pinch of salt
4 to 5 tablespoons ice water
1 egg white beaten with 1 teaspoon water

FILLING
10 ounces fresh spinach, washed, stems removed
2 tablespoons olive oil
1 clove garlic, minced

1 small onion, finely diced
1 cup chopped fresh wild mushrooms (shiitake, chanterelle, or oyster, about 6 ounces)
2 tablespoons pine nuts, toasted
1 bunch (about 4 ounces) arugula, washed, dried, and chopped
Pinch of ground nutmeg
Salt and pepper
1 small package (3 ounces) cream cheese, softened
2/3 cup sour cream
3 eggs
1/3 cup grated Parmesan cheese

1. *Prepare tart dough and shell:* Cut the butter and shortening into very small pieces and place in the freezer for 1 hour.
2. Place the flour and salt in a food processor, add the chilled butter and shortening, and process until the mixture is the consistency of coarse meal, about 30 seconds. With the motor running, slowly add the water and process just until the dough starts to form a ball. Gather the dough together and press it into a circle; cover with plastic wrap and allow to rest at room temperature for 1 hour.
3. Roll out the dough on a floured worktable, then press it into a 10-inch tart pan with a removable bottom. Refrigerate the tart shell for 1 hour.
4. Preheat the oven to 375°. Line the tart shell with aluminum foil and fill it with pie weights or dried beans. Bake the shell for 20 minutes. Remove the foil and weights, brush the bottom of the shell with the egg white mixture, and continue to bake until lightly browned, about 10 minutes. Remove from the oven and set aside.
5. *Prepare the filling:* Steam or boil the spinach until wilted, about 2 minutes. Drain well and squeeze out any excess liquid. Finely chop the spinach and set aside.

6. Heat the olive oil in a large skillet over medium-high heat. Add the garlic and cook just until it starts to brown. Add the onion and mushrooms, reduce the heat to medium, and cook for 5 minutes, stirring often. Stir in the chopped spinach, pine nuts, arugula, and nutmeg, season with salt and pepper, and cook for 1 minute more. Remove from heat and set aside to cool.
7. Combine the cream cheese and sour cream in the bowl of an electric mixer. Using a paddle attachment, mix on low speed until smooth, scraping down the sides of the bowl when necessary. Add the eggs one at a time and mix just until combined. Stir in the spinach mixture and the Parmesan cheese.
8. Pour the filling into the tart shell and bake until a knife inserted near the center comes out clean, about 20 to 25 minutes. Serve warm or at room temperature.

COUNTRY BISCUITS

Makes 12 to 15 biscuits

These biscuits make a splendid breakfast when topped with Tomato Welsh Rarebit (page 3) and are wonderful by themselves. For a more tender and flaky biscuit, gently and briefly knead the dough. The scraps left over from cutting the biscuits can be gathered together, rolled out, and cut into more biscuits.

1 package active dry yeast (2¼ teaspoons)	1 tablespoon baking powder
½ cup warm water	1 teaspoon salt
1 tablespoon plus 1 teaspoon sugar	¼ pound unsalted butter
4 cups all-purpose flour	1 cup buttermilk
	Light cream for brushing tops

1. Preheat the oven to 400°.
2. In a small bowl combine the yeast, water, and the 1 *teaspoon* sugar. Let stand for 10 minutes.
3. In a large bowl blend together the flour, baking powder, the 1 tablespoon sugar, and the salt. Cut the butter into the flour mixture using your fingertips or a pastry cutter until the mixture resembles coarse crumbs. Stir in the yeast mixture and buttermilk and blend just until the dough forms. Do not overmix.
4. Place the dough on a lightly floured surface and knead for 6 to 8 strokes. Roll out or pat the dough with your fingertips to a 1-inch thickness. Cut the biscuits with a 2½-inch round cutter or a heart-shaped cutter. Transfer the biscuits to an ungreased baking pan and let rest for 15 minutes.
5. Brush the tops of the biscuits with the light cream and bake until golden, about 20 minutes. Serve warm.

LEMON POPPY SEED CAKE

Serves 16

This is a wonderful cake for those who enjoy something sweet for breakfast. Using cake flour gives it a light, delicate texture. This cake keeps well in the refrigerator or freezer.

¾ pound unsalted butter, softened
1¾ cups sugar
6 eggs, separated
½ cup poppy seeds
2 tablespoons grated lemon zest
1 tablespoon grated orange zest

2¼ cups cake flour, sifted
Pinch of salt

LEMON GLAZE
⅓ cup lemon juice
3 tablespoons sugar

1. Preheat the oven to 350°. Grease and lightly flour a 10-inch fluted tube pan.
2. Using an electric mixer with a paddle attachment, beat the butter for 30 seconds. Gradually add 1½ cups of the sugar; mix on medium-high speed until light and fluffy, about 2 to 3 minutes. Reduce the speed to medium-low; add the egg yolks one at a time, scraping down the bowl when necessary. Stir in the poppy seeds and zests. Stir in the flour and salt just until combined. The batter will be thick.
3. In a separate bowl, beat egg whites with the whip attachment of an electric mixer until soft peaks form. Slowly add the remaining ¼ cup sugar and continue to beat until stiff peaks form.
4. Fold 1 cup of the beaten egg whites into the poppy seed batter to lighten it. Fold the remaining whites into the batter just until combined.
5. Transfer the batter to the pan and bake until a toothpick inserted near the center comes out clean, about 1 hour.
6. Let the cake cool on a wire rack for 10 minutes. Remove the cake from the pan and poke holes in the top with a toothpick while the cake is still warm.
7. *Prepare the lemon glaze:* In a small saucepan combine the lemon juice and sugar. Cook over medium heat until the sugar dissolves and the mixture comes to a boil. Let the glaze cool slightly, then spoon it over the cake. Serve warm or at room temperature.

Breakfast from Joan Schlosstein

We met Joan Schlosstein in 1990 when she responded to our *Boston Globe* ad seeking a breakfast cook and baker. Though we're always hopeful such arrangements will develop into long-term relationships, seldom have we been so rewarded by friendship.

Joan had been an environmental chemistry researcher and was looking for a change. We were impressed by her personality and willingness to take the bold step of launching a new career. Soon, it became clear that the limited time she had spent in a kitchen, as part-time assistant to a caterer, had been put to good use. She was an outstanding baker and, from the first year, she and Terry have worked together to create a very enticing breakfast formula. In addition to each day's pastry, whether it be Joan's unparalleled sticky buns or her ginger scones, she offers a menu of breakfast favorites that are delicious, nutritious, and attractive.

During Joan's first year here, she experienced a chemical reaction that changed her life. At our end-of-season party, she was attracted to the saxophonist playing in the band. The feeling turned out to be mutual and, a year later, she married Kit Loekle, a boat-builder by day, and a musician, gardener, birder, vintner, animal husbandman by night and weekend. They now live just a mile from the Inn. Together they have created extraordinary gardens, which seem to double in size every year. Each day before Joan walks to work, she tours her gardens and chooses the fresh herbs and flowers she'll incorporate in that morning's breakfast. Perhaps it's these home-grown ingredients, combined with her background in chemistry, that, in her words, "make breakfast a thrill to prepare."
                                                            —*Jean and Dud Hendrick*

JOAN'S GINGER SCONES

Makes 15 to 18 scones

Traditionally served with afternoon tea, scones are now being offered at many tables with eggs, country sausage, and fresh fruit for a simple but tasty breakfast. Scones can be made round as described here, shaped into a circle and cut into wedges like a pie, or shaped into a rectangle and cut into squares.

4 cups all-purpose flour
¼ cup cornstarch
1 tablespoon grated fresh ginger
1½ teaspoons grated lemon zest
1½ teaspoons grated orange zest
½ teaspoon salt
4½ teaspoons baking powder
½ teaspoon baking soda

¼ cup sugar
½ pound unsalted butter, softened
1 cup heavy cream
1 teaspoon lemon juice
1 egg yolk
2 tablespoons milk
Sugar for sprinkling

1. Preheat the oven to 375°.
2. Place the flour, cornstarch, ginger, lemon and orange zest, salt, baking powder, baking soda, and sugar in a food processor and process for 10 seconds. Add the butter in small pieces and process until the mixture resembles coarse meal. Slowly add the cream and lemon juice and process just until dough forms.
3. Turn the dough out onto a well-floured surface and knead for 10 to 12 strokes. Roll or press it out to a ½-inch to ¾-inch thickness; cut the scones with a 3-inch round cutter. Knead the scraps together, reroll, and cut into more scones.
4. Mix the egg yolk and milk together and brush the tops of the scones. Sprinkle lightly with sugar and bake until golden brown, about 15 minutes. Serve warm or at room temperature.

JOAN'S ZUCCHINI NUT BREAD

Makes 2 loaves

This sweet, moist bread is easy to make and keeps well in the refrigerator or freezer. When selecting zucchini, choose those that are small to medium in size; large ones can be bitter. Also, select zucchini that are firm and have a smooth, glossy appearance. Do not peel the zucchini—the skin adds flavor and color—and do not squeeze the moisture out of the grated zucchini before using it.

3 cups all-purpose flour
1½ teaspoons ground cinnamon
1 teaspoon baking soda
½ teaspoon baking powder
½ teaspoon salt
3 eggs

2 cups sugar
1 cup vegetable oil
1 teaspoon vanilla extract
2 cups grated zucchini (2 to 3 medium zucchini)
½ cup chopped toasted walnuts

1. Preheat the oven to 350°. Grease and flour two 9- by 5-inch loaf pans.
2. In a large mixing bowl combine the flour, cinnamon, baking soda, baking powder, and salt.
3. In a medium bowl beat together the eggs, sugar, oil, and vanilla. Stir into the flour mixture just until combined. Fold in the zucchini and walnuts.
4. Pour the batter into the prepared pans. Bake until a toothpick inserted near the center comes out clean, about 50 to 60 minutes. Remove from the oven and let cool for 10 minutes. Remove the loaves from the pans and let cool completely on a wire rack before serving.

JOAN'S BLUEBERRY CORNMEAL MUFFINS

Makes 24 muffins

Cornmeal fans will love the flavor of these blueberry muffins, wonderful when served with honey butter. Remember to gently fold in the ingredients and not to overmix the batter, so the muffins will be light and tender.

2¼ cups all-purpose flour
1 cup plus 2 tablespoons cornmeal
¾ cup sugar
4½ teaspoons baking powder
3 eggs

5 tablespoons unsalted butter, melted
1½ cups buttermilk
1 cup blueberries

1. Preheat the oven to 375°. Grease twenty-four 2½-inch muffin cups or line them with paper baking cups.
2. In a large bowl combine the flour, cornmeal, sugar, and baking powder. In a small bowl whisk together the eggs, butter, and buttermilk; gently stir into the dry ingredients just until combined.
3. Gently fold in the blueberries. Fill the prepared muffin tins three-quarters full. Bake until a toothpick inserted near the center comes out clean, about 25 to 30 minutes. Allow to cool on a wire rack. Serve warm or at room temperature.

GRANOLA

Makes about 6 cups

For the cold cereal enthusiast, this makes a satisfying breakfast. It is also a delicious light midday snack. This granola keeps well and has much more flavor and freshness than any you can buy. It is also considerably less expensive than the store-bought variety.

2 cups rolled oats
½ cup wheat germ
½ cup wheat bran
½ cup sunflower seeds
¼ cup sesame seeds
½ cup sliced almonds
½ cup unsweetened flaked coconut

2 teaspoons ground cinnamon
¼ cup vegetable oil
¼ cup honey
2 tablespoons water
1 teaspoon molasses or brown sugar
1 teaspoon vanilla extract
¼ cup raisins

1. Preheat the oven to 325°.
2. Combine the oats, wheat germ, wheat bran, sunflower seeds, sesame seeds, almonds, coconut, and cinnamon in a large bowl.
3. Heat the oil, honey, water, molasses, and vanilla extract in a saucepan over medium-low heat until dissolved, stirring often. Stir into the dry ingredients and mix well.
4. Transfer the mixture to a baking pan. Bake until lightly browned and dry, about 1 hour, stirring every 15 minutes. Remove from the oven and allow to cool completely. Stir in the raisins. Serve, or store in an airtight container.

REBEKAH RAYE'S SWEET ROLLS

Makes 24 rolls

Fresh from the oven, these rolls have a wonderful aroma and are a superb way to start the day. They are rich and flavorful, with a lovely caramel glaze. Leftover rolls, if there are any, make an excellent bread pudding.

3 packages active dry yeast
½ cup warm water
2 cups milk
4 tablespoons unsalted butter
1 cup plus 2 tablespoons
  granulated sugar
Pinch of salt

5 to 6 cups all-purpose flour
1 cup firmly packed brown sugar
2 teaspoons ground cinnamon
¾ cup raisins
¾ cup walnut pieces, toasted and
  chopped
¼ pound unsalted butter, melted

1. In a small bowl combine the yeast and the water. Let stand 10 minutes.
2. Heat the milk, the 4 tablespoons butter, the 2 tablespoons sugar, and the salt in a small saucepan over low heat. Cook until the butter is melted, about 2 minutes, stirring occasionally. Allow to cool.
3. Transfer the mixture to a mixing bowl. Add the yeast mixture along with 2 cups of the flour; stir until smooth. Continue to stir in flour until the dough starts to come together and forms a ball.
4. Transfer the dough to a floured worktable. Knead the dough, adding more flour when necessary to prevent sticking, until the dough is smooth and firm, about 10 minutes. Transfer the dough to a greased bowl; cover and refrigerate overnight.
5. Remove the dough from the refrigerator; punch down the dough and let it rise in a warm place (80° to 90°) for 30 minutes.
6. Meanwhile, combine the brown sugar, the 1 cup granulated sugar, the cinnamon, raisins, and walnuts in a small bowl. Set aside.
7. Divide the dough in half. Roll out half the dough into an 18- by 10-inch rectangle about ½ inch thick. Brush half the melted butter over the dough. Sprinkle half the brown sugar mixture over the dough, then roll it up jelly-roll style, beginning with a long side. Seal the seams, then cut the roll into twelve 1½-inch rounds using a serrated knife.
8. Grease twenty-four 2½-inch muffin cups or line them with paper baking cups. Place the rounds, cut side down, in the prepared tins. Repeat with the remaining dough, melted butter, and brown sugar mixture. Cover and let rise in a warm place (80° to 90°) until the rolls almost double in size, about 30 minutes.
9. Preheat the oven to 375°. Bake the rolls until golden brown, 25 to 30 minutes. Let cool slightly, then remove from the pans and serve warm.

PUMPKIN MUFFINS

Makes 24 muffins

These are excellent morning muffins with a delicate pumpkin flavor. They are easy to make and a good choice to serve during the holiday season.

1 can (15 ounces) pumpkin purée
2 cups sugar
¾ cup vegetable oil
3 eggs
½ cup water
2¾ cups all-purpose flour

1½ teaspoons baking powder
1 teaspoon baking soda
Pinch of salt
1 teaspoon ground nutmeg
1½ teaspoons ground cinnamon

1. Preheat the oven to 350°. Grease twenty-four 2½-inch muffin cups or line them with paper baking cups.
2. In a large bowl stir together the pumpkin, sugar, oil, eggs, and water until well blended.
3. Sift together the remaining ingredients into another bowl; stir into the pumpkin mixture just until combined, being careful not to overmix.
4. Divide the batter among the prepared tins. Bake until a toothpick inserted near the center comes out clean, about 20 to 30 minutes. Allow the muffins to cool on a wire rack. Serve warm or at room temperature.

HORS D'OEUVRES

SESAME GINGER MUSSELS

Serves 4

This is the most requested recipe from Pilgrim's Inn. Cook the mussels only long enough to open the shells; overcooking will make the mussels tough. You can substitute littleneck clams if mussels are not available. Pickled ginger can be found in the Asian food section of most well-stocked supermarkets.

24 mussels, debearded and scrubbed
½ cup dry white wine
1 teaspoon chopped fresh ginger
1 clove garlic, minced
2 ounces pickled ginger

MARINADE
½ cup soy sauce
½ cup peanut oil

Few drops sesame oil
1 teaspoon rice wine vinegar
Pinch of sugar
1 teaspoon Dijon mustard
2 teaspoons chopped fresh ginger
2 tablespoons chopped fresh cilantro
2 tablespoons chopped fresh parsley
1 red onion, finely diced

1. Place the mussels, wine, fresh ginger, and garlic in a large saucepan. Cover and cook over medium-high heat, shaking the pan every few minutes, until all the mussels have opened, about 6 to 8 minutes. Remove from heat and allow to cool.
2. Meanwhile, prepare the marinade: In a stainless steel bowl combine all the marinade ingredients and whisk until blended. Set aside until needed.
3. Discard any mussels that have not opened. Remove the mussels from the shells; reserve the shells. Place the mussels in the marinade and stir to coat thoroughly. Cover with plastic wrap and allow to marinate at room temperature for 1 hour.
4. Place one mussel in each shell along with a little of the marinade. Top each mussel with a slice of the pickled ginger and serve.

Mussels from Jack Hamblen

To say Jack Hamblen is colorful and larger than life isn't quite adequate. Full of warmth and personality, he arrives in our kitchen early in the morning with a bucket of mussels and a story delivered in a booming Downeast accent. At the age of seven, he began clamming, earning 35 cents a bushel to buy his first bicycle—with wooden wheels! Now in his seventies, he still has the energy of a young fisherman.

In addition to fishing, for several years Jack was a produce salesman on the island and, in response to his wife's urging that he get a job with steady pay, he was the town's dump attendant for eight years—at $10 per week.

After many years, Jack gave up fishing, but he's still involved in the business. His son, Jack, Jr., now supplies him the mussels that he delivers to Terry for our most-appreciated hors d'oeuvre: Sesame Ginger Mussels. Jack's smoked and pickled mussels are in high demand, and his many other interests make him legitimately a "Jack" of all trades. In addition to his smokehouse work, Jack grows prize-winning vegetables and is an accomplished woodcarver. He shares his creations with family and friends, and it's a rare visit that we're not the grateful recipients of some gift. Yet, it is his generosity of spirit we most appreciate. After his departure from our kitchen, we are smiling and more able to deal with our own lives by thinking about Jack's exuberance in his.

—*Jean and Dud Hendrick*

CHICKEN LIVER AND SUN-DRIED CHERRY PÂTÉ

Serves 8

This is a particularly fine and moist pâté with a rich flavor. Its subtle sweetness is enhanced by the sun-dried cherries. Duck livers can be substituted for the chicken livers. The pâté should be prepared in advance to allow the flavors to mellow.

¾ cup sun-dried cherries
¼ cup Cognac
2 tablespoons duck fat or unsalted butter
2 shallots, minced
¾ pound chicken livers, trimmed, rinsed, and patted dry

Salt and pepper
Pinch of cardamom
¼ pound unsalted butter, softened
½ teaspoon lemon juice

Crackers for accompaniment

1. Soak the cherries in the Cognac for 1 hour to plump them.
2. Heat the duck fat in a large skillet over medium heat. Add the shallot and sauté for 1 minute. Add the livers and season with salt and pepper. Add the cardamom and sauté until the livers are pink inside, about 4 to 5 minutes.
3. Pour in the cherries and Cognac and cook for 1 minute. Remove from heat and allow to cool completely.
4. Place the liver mixture in a food processor and purée for 30 seconds. Scrape down the bowl and process for another 30 seconds. Add the butter and lemon juice; purée until smooth and well blended.
5. Transfer the pâté to a ramekin, serving bowl, or crock. Cover with plastic wrap and refrigerate for 4 hours or overnight. Serve with crackers.

BRUSCHETTA WITH SALMON

Serves 6

Bruschetta are slices of hearty country bread grilled over a fire, rubbed with garlic, and topped with various combinations of herbs, vegetables, meats, and seafood. Simple, satisfying, and rustic, bruschetta make excellent hors d'oeuvres, antipasti, or garnish for salads. The salmon in this dish can be prepared in advance; however, the topping should be placed on the grilled bread as close to serving time as possible to prevent the bread from becoming soggy.

½ pound salmon fillet
3 tablespoons olive oil
6 3- by 4-inch slices Italian or French
  bread, cut ½ inch thick
2 cloves garlic, cut in half
1 small red bell pepper, finely diced
2 scallions, thinly sliced

1 tablespoon chopped fresh dill
1 tablespoon chopped fresh parsley
Juice of 1 lime
1 tablespoon mayonnaise
Salt and pepper

6 sprigs fresh dill for garnish

1. Prepare a charcoal grill.
2. Brush the salmon with 1 tablespoon of the olive oil; grill over a medium-high fire just until done, 3 to 4 minutes per side. Set aside to cool.
3. Rub the bread slices with the cut side of the garlic. Brush the slices with 2 tablespoons of the olive oil and grill until light brown on both sides. Set aside.
4. Flake the grilled salmon and place in a bowl. Stir in the bell pepper, scallion, chopped dill, parsley, lime juice, and mayonnaise. Season with salt and pepper and mix until well blended.
5. To serve, spoon the salmon mixture on top of each bread slice and garnish with a sprig of dill.

BRUSCHETTA WITH TOMATOES, ARUGULA, AND MAINE CRAB

Serves 6

At the height of tomato season, this makes an excellent hors d'oeuvre. It is essential to pair fresh, vine-ripened tomatoes with a good-quality olive oil. For a tasty variation, substitute chopped fresh basil for the arugula and sprinkle a little grated Parmesan cheese on top.

6 3- by 4-inch slices Italian or French
   bread, cut ½ inch thick
1 clove garlic, cut in half
¼ cup olive oil
2 tomatoes, peeled, seeded, and diced

½ cup chopped arugula
Ground black pepper
6 ounces crabmeat
2 tablespoons lemon juice

1. Prepare a charcoal grill or preheat the broiler.
2. Rub the bread slices with the cut side of the garlic, brush with the olive oil, and grill or broil until lightly browned on both sides.
3. Stir together the tomato and arugula in a bowl. Season with black pepper and place on top of the bread slices.
4. Arrange the crab on top of the tomato mixture and drizzle a little lemon juice over each bruschetta. Serve immediately.

CROSTINI WITH GRILLED EGGPLANT AND ROASTED GARLIC

Serves 6

Crostini and bruschetta are two resourceful ways to use leftover, slightly stale bread. Crostini is much like bruschetta except that the toppings are usually more refined. They may be coarsely ground, puréed, or simply diced fine. For convenience, the bread can be toasted or pan-fried in olive oil instead of grilled. This crostini dish captures a hint of smokiness from the charcoal grill and is complemented by the flavorful combination of eggplant, garlic, and balsamic vinegar. It would be an ideal choice as a first course for a lamb dinner.

1 bulb garlic
5 tablespoons olive oil
1 medium eggplant
6 3- by 4-inch slices Italian or French
   bread, cut ½ inch thick
1 teaspoon balsamic vinegar

1 tablespoon chopped fresh parsley
1 tablespoon chopped fresh basil
Salt and pepper

Black olives for garnish
Grated Parmesan cheese for garnish

1. Preheat the oven to 300°.
2. Rub the garlic with 1 tablespoon of the olive oil. Place in a small roasting pan, cover with aluminum foil, and bake for 1 hour.
3. Remove the garlic from the oven and allow to cool for 30 minutes. Meanwhile, prepare a charcoal grill.
4. Peel the eggplant and cut into ½-inch slices. Brush both sides with olive oil and grill until lightly browned on both sides, about 2 to 3 minutes per side. Set aside to cool.
5. Brush the bread slices with olive oil and grill until browned on both sides. Set aside.
6. Cut a ½-inch slice off the top of the baked garlic bulb using a serrated knife. Squeeze the soft garlic into a food processor. Add the grilled eggplant, vinegar, parsley, and basil. Season with salt and pepper and process to a smooth paste.
7. Spread the paste onto the grilled bread slices and garnish with chopped black olives and Parmesan cheese. Serve immediately.

HERB-MARINATED MOZZARELLA

Serves 4

This simple, easy hors d'oeuvre works well on an antipasti plate. It can be prepared well in advance and refrigerated until needed. Bring to room temperature before serving. Any leftovers would make a delicious topping for pizza.

¼ cup olive oil
½ red onion, finely diced
1 tablespoon chopped fresh basil
2 tablespoons chopped fresh chives
1 tablespoon chopped fresh thyme
1 tablespoon chopped fresh parsley

Salt and pepper
1 pound mozzarella cheese, cut into 1-inch cubes

Crackers or sliced focaccia for accompaniment

1. Stir together the oil, onion, and herbs in a bowl and season with salt and pepper. Add the mozzarella and stir to coat the cheese. Cover and let stand at room temperature for 1 hour.
2. Place the cheese on a serving platter and serve with crackers or slices of focaccia.

BAKED BRIE WITH HAZELNUTS

Serves 4

There is something incredibly satisfying about spreading and eating warm cheese on a cracker or slice of apple. This is a convenient dish for the busy cook; it is easy to make and can be prepared the day before. Bring the cheese to room temperature before baking.

½ cup hazelnuts, toasted and finely diced
2 tablespoons bread crumbs
1 round (8 ounces) Brie cheese
1 egg, beaten

Fresh fruit and crackers for accompaniment

1. Stir together the nuts and bread crumbs.
2. Slice a very thin layer off the top of the Brie. Brush the top with the egg, top with the nut mixture, and chill for 1 hour.
3. Preheat the oven to 350°. Place the cheese on a roasting pan and bake until slightly warm, about 10 minutes (take care not to let the cheese melt). Serve immediately with fresh fruit and crackers.

PECAN AND CAMEMBERT CANAPÉS

Serves 4

This unusual combination is absolutely delicious. Almost any cracker will work fine in this dish; however, the black pepper gives a nice bite that complements the richness of the cheese and butter mixture.

¼ pound unsalted butter, softened
1 tablespoon honey
12 cracked black pepper crackers

1 round (8 ounces) Camembert,
  cut into 12 wedges
12 pecan halves, toasted

1. Stir together the butter and honey in a small bowl.
2. Spread about ½ teaspoon of the butter mixture on each cracker. Top with a wedge of Camembert. Place a small amount of the butter mixture on top of the Camembert and top with a pecan half. Serve immediately.

TAPENADE

About 1 cup

A simple olive paste, tapenade is often called "poor man's caviar" or "black butter." It can be served as a dip with focaccia or crudités, tossed with pasta, used in a filling for ravioli, or spread on a slice of crusty Italian bread for crostini.

1 small bulb garlic
⅓ cup plus 1 tablespoon olive oil
2 generous cups Kalamata olives, pitted
1 tablespoon capers

1 teaspoon chopped fresh thyme
Juice of 1 lemon
Pinch of ground black pepper

1. Preheat the oven to 300°.
2. Coat the garlic with the 1 *tablespoon* olive oil and place in a small roasting pan. Cover with aluminum foil and bake for 1 hour.
3. Remove the garlic from the oven and allow to cool for 30 minutes.
4. Cut a ½-inch slice off the top of the baked garlic bulb using a serrated knife. Squeeze the soft garlic into a food processor. Add the ⅓ cup olive oil, the olives, capers, thyme, lemon juice, and black pepper; purée until smooth. Serve at room temperature

POLENTA CANAPÉS WITH TAPENADE

Makes 16 to 20 canapés

This easy-to-make hors d'oeuvre can be prepared well in advance. The polenta may be grilled once it has been chilled and before spreading on the tapenade. Lightly brush the polenta with olive oil and place it on a hot grill for 1 to 2 minutes.

2 cups Chicken Stock (page 138)
   or Vegetable Stock (page 140)
1 tablespoon olive oil
½ cup instant polenta
3 ounces fontina cheese, cut into
   small cubes

¼ cup grated Parmesan cheese
Salt and pepper
½ to ¾ cup Tapenade (page 23)
½ red bell pepper, thinly sliced

1. Combine the stock and olive oil in a small saucepan and bring to a boil. Slowly whisk in the polenta and return to a boil. Reduce the heat to medium-low and cook for 5 minutes, stirring constantly.
2. Remove from heat and stir in the fontina and Parmesan until the cheeses are melted and smooth. Season with salt and pepper.
3. Lightly grease an 8-inch-square pan or other baking pan. Pour the mixture into the square pan (if using a baking pan, spread the mixture to a ½-inch thickness). Allow to cool at room temperature for 30 minutes, then refrigerate for 1 hour.
4. Spread a thin layer of tapenade over the polenta. Cut into 1½-inch squares or circles or any shape desired. Garnish the tops with the slices of bell pepper. Serve at room temperature or slightly warmed.

HUMMUS WITH GOAT CHEESE

Makes about 3 cups

This smooth spread with its earthy, nutty flavor works well as a dip with tortilla chips or crackers, as a filling for pita bread, on a sandwich with grilled eggplant and tomato, or as part of a composed salad. Adjust the seasoning as desired.

1 cup dried garbanzo beans	4 tablespoons olive oil
Salt and pepper	1 teaspoon ground cumin
2 cloves garlic, minced	1 teaspoon ground coriander
Few drops sesame oil	2 tablespoons chopped fresh parsley
Juice and grated zest of 2 lemons	3 ounces goat cheese, softened

1. Soak the beans in water for 24 hours.
2. Drain the beans. Cover with fresh water and add a pinch of salt. Bring to a boil, reduce the heat, and simmer slowly until the beans are soft, about 1 hour.
3. Drain the beans again, reserving ¼ cup of the cooking liquid. Place the beans in a food processor with the garlic, sesame oil, lemon juice and zest, olive oil, spices, parsley, cheese, and the reserved cooking liquid. Season with salt and pepper; purée until smooth. Check the seasoning and serve.

ROASTED EGGPLANT DIP

Makes about 1½ cups

Preparing this dip ahead and chilling it for up to 3 days allow the flavors to develop and intensify. The dip can be served with focaccia, crackers, or pita bread, spread on cucumber rounds, or used as a topping for crostini.

1 bulb garlic	1 teaspoon ground cumin
1 tablespoon olive oil	½ teaspoon ground turmeric
1 large eggplant	3 tablespoons chopped fresh cilantro
Juice of 1 lime	Pinch of cayenne pepper
½ teaspoon sesame oil	Salt and pepper

1. Preheat the oven to 300°.
2. Place the garlic in a small roasting pan, brush with the olive oil, cover with aluminum foil, and bake for 1 hour.
3. Meanwhile, prick the eggplant all over with a fork and place in another roasting pan. Bake until soft, about 40 to 50 minutes. Remove from the oven and allow to cool.
4. Remove the garlic from the oven and allow to cool.
5. Peel the eggplant and place the pulp in a food processor. Add the olive oil left in the roasting pan from the garlic. Cut a ½-inch slice off the top of the garlic bulb and squeeze the soft garlic into the processor. Add the remaining ingredients and purée until smooth.
6. Check the seasoning and serve the dip chilled or at room temperature.

ARTICHOKE DIP

Serves 8 to 10

At Pilgrim's Inn we use a fondue set to keep this dip warm during cocktail hour. The dip can be made a few hours in advance, then covered and refrigerated until needed. Allow about an hour to bring it to room temperature before baking.

2 teaspoons lemon juice
4 cups water
10 fresh baby artichokes
1 cup dry white wine
½ cup mayonnaise
¼ cup grated Parmesan cheese
1 tablespoon chopped fresh parsley
1 egg plus 1 egg yolk

1 teaspoon Dijon mustard
1 tablespoon chopped fresh chives
Dash of Tabasco and
   Worcestershire sauce
Salt and pepper

Crackers for accompaniment

1. Mix 1 teaspoon of the lemon juice with the water in a bowl.
2. Cut off the stem and ¼ inch of the top of each artichoke. Peel away the tough outer leaves to expose the yellow leaves. Cut each artichoke in half and remove the choke. Place the artichokes in the bowl of lemon water.
3. Drain the artichokes and place in a saucepan with the wine and enough water to cover. Bring to a boil; reduce the heat and simmer until the artichokes are tender, about 20 minutes. Drain well and allow to cool.
4. Transfer the artichokes to a food processor and add the remaining ingredients. Purée until smooth.
5. Preheat the oven to 350°.
6. Transfer the artichoke mixture to two 6- or 8-ounce ramekins. Bake until set and lightly browned, about 30 to 40 minutes. Serve warm with crackers.

NORI-ROLLED SUSHI WITH LOBSTER

Serves 8 to 10

This festive and impressive hors d'oeuvre is ideal for a large party. Once you are familiar with the rolling technique, you will find these easy to prepare. The fillings for nori rolls are endless; use your imagination and have fun. Try to make the nori rolls as close to serving time as possible; they do not keep well in the refrigerator. The nori sheets, wasabi powder, tamari soy sauce, pickled ginger, and rolling mat can be found in the Asian section of some well-stocked supermarkets or in Asian food stores.

1 lobster (1½ pounds)
1 cup rice
1 tablespoon rice wine vinegar
1 teaspoon sugar
2 teaspoons wasabi powder
    plus more for serving
4 or 5 nori sheets

2 scallions, cut into thin strips
¼ cup chopped fresh cilantro
¼ cup chopped pickled ginger plus
    more for serving
¼ cup tamari soy sauce plus more
    for serving

1. Steam or boil the lobster for 10 minutes. Remove from heat and allow to cool.
2. Remove the lobster meat and discard the shells. Cut the meat into strips about ¼ inch wide and set aside.
3. Cook the rice. Remove from heat and stir in the vinegar and the sugar. Spread the rice onto a baking pan and let cool to room temperature, tossing it occasionally with 2 forks to hasten the cooling.
4. Mix the wasabi with enough water to form a loose paste; set aside.
5. Place 1 nori sheet on a bamboo rolling mat. Dampen your hands and spread about ¾ cup of the cooked rice over the nori, leaving a 1-inch strip at the top edge uncovered.
6. About 2 inches up from the bottom of the nori, place a few strips of lobster meat and scallion across the rice, extending from one side of the sheet to the other. Spread a very thin layer of wasabi paste over the lobster and scallion. Sprinkle with some of the cilantro and top with a few pieces of pickled ginger.
7. Lightly moisten the exposed top edge of the nori with water. Tightly roll up the mixture using the rolling mat, starting at the bottom edge. Repeat with the remaining nori and other ingredients.
8. Use a sharp knife to trim away the rough ends of each roll, then slice each roll into 1-inch rounds. Arrange the rounds on a serving plate. Serve with separate bowls of tamari, pickled ginger, and wasabi paste.

PIZZA WITH LEEKS, ROSEMARY, AND BLUE CHEESE

Makes two 10-inch pizzas

1 recipe Pizza Dough (page 144)
3 tablespoons olive oil
4 small leeks, cleaned and finely sliced
Cornmeal for dusting paddle

2 tablespoons chopped fresh rosemary
5 ounces blue cheese, crumbled
6 ounces fresh mozzarella cheese, thinly sliced
Salt and pepper

1. Prepare the pizza dough and set aside.
2. Heat 1 tablespoon of the olive oil in a large sauté pan over medium heat. Add the leeks and sauté for 4 to 5 minutes, stirring often. Set aside.
3. Preheat the oven with a pizza stone inside to 475°.
4. Place the pizza dough on a floured worktable. Using your fingertips press the dough into a circle 10 to 12 inches in diameter and about ¼ inch thick. Transfer the dough to a wooden paddle dusted with cornmeal. Brush the dough with 1 tablespoon of the olive oil, top with half of the leeks, half the rosemary, and half the cheeses. Season with salt and pepper.
5. Make sure that the dough is loose from the paddle, then slide it onto the pizza stone. Bake the pizza until lightly browned, about 10 to 15 minutes. Remove from the oven and repeat with the remaining dough, olive oil, and topping ingredients. Serve hot.

ABOUT PIZZA

I find that pressing the pizza dough into a circle with my fingertips instead of using a rolling pin results in a much softer and more tender crust. Don't try to press out a perfect circle; an uneven shape and thickness gives the pizza more of a rustic appearance. The dough may also be shaped for small individual pizzas, which can be paired with a garden salad for a satisfying lunch.

One of the best ways to cook a pizza is on a pizza stone. When pizza is placed on an extremely hot stone, the dough immediately starts to cook, which prevents the toppings from saturating the dough thus ensuring a crispy crust. Use a wooden paddle to place the pizza in and to remove it from the oven. Remember to lightly dust the paddle with cornmeal (flour does not work as well) before placing the pizza on it. This will make it easier to slide the pizza off the paddle and onto the stone.

When creating your own pizza toppings, keep the amount of topping on the light side. Too much weight on the pizza dough may keep the dough from properly rising and result in a dense and chewy crust. Remember that the toppings will be in the oven only for a brief cooking time (10 to 15 minutes), so most vegetables should be partially sautéed or blanched beforehand.

PIZZA WITH ROASTED RED PEPPERS, TOMATO, AND CILANTRO

Makes two 10-inch pizzas

1 recipe Pizza Dough (page 144)
4 red bell peppers, roasted
3 tablespoons olive oil
3 small onions, finely diced
4 cloves garlic, minced
2 jalapeño peppers, minced
Cornmeal for dusting paddle
6 tablespoons chopped fresh cilantro

4 tablespoons chopped fresh parsley
2 tomatoes, peeled, seeded, and
  finely diced
6 ounces fresh mozzarella cheese,
  thinly sliced
6 ounces fontina cheese, cut into
  ½-inch cubes
Salt and pepper

1. Prepare the pizza dough and set aside.
2. Place the peppers over a charcoal grill, under the broiler, or over a gas flame. Roast until the skin is uniformly charred, turning the peppers as needed. Place the peppers in a plastic bag, seal tightly, and allow to steam for 30 minutes. Remove the peppers from the bag, peel away the skin, cut the peppers in half, and discard the seeds and stems. Finely dice the peppers and set aside.
3. Heat 1 tablespoon of the olive oil over medium-high heat in a sauté pan. Add the onion, garlic, and jalapeño pepper; sauté until soft, about 4 to 5 minutes, stirring occasionally. Set aside.
4. Preheat the oven with a pizza stone inside to 475°.
5. Place the pizza dough on a floured worktable. Using your fingertips press the dough into a circle 10 to 12 inches in diameter and about ¼ inch thick. Transfer the dough to a wooden paddle dusted with cornmeal. Brush the dough with 1 tablespoon of the olive oil, then top with half of the onion mixture, half the herbs, half the roasted bell pepper, half the tomato, and half the cheeses. Season with salt and pepper.
6. Make sure that the dough is loose from the paddle, then slide the pizza onto the stone. Bake the pizza until lightly browned, 10 to 15 minutes. Remove from the oven and repeat with the remaining dough, olive oil, and topping ingredients. Serve hot.

PIZZA WITH RADICCHIO, CAPERS, AND BLACK OLIVES

Makes two 10-inch pizzas

Radicchio is an Italian chicory with a strong and pleasantly bitter flavor. It may be grilled before adding it to the topping for this pizza. To grill radicchio, cut the head into quarters, brush the quarters with olive oil, season with salt and pepper, and cook over a low charcoal fire for 3 to 5 minutes. Remove the sections from the grill and slice them into very fine ribbons.

1 recipe Pizza Dough (page 144)
2 strips bacon, diced
2 cloves garlic, minced
1 red bell pepper, thinly sliced
1 head radicchio, thinly sliced
Cornmeal for dusting paddle

2 tablespoons capers
½ cup chopped black olives
12 ounces fontina cheese, cut
　　into ½-inch cubes
Ground black pepper

1. Prepare the pizza dough and set aside.
2. Cook the bacon in a large skillet over medium heat until crisp. Add the garlic and bell pepper and cook for 3 to 4 minutes, stirring often. Stir in the radicchio and cook for 2 to 3 minutes. Set aside.
3. Preheat the oven with a pizza stone inside to 475°.
4. Place the pizza dough on a floured worktable. Using your fingertips press the dough into a circle 10 to 12 inches in diameter and about ¼ inch thick. Transfer the dough to a wooden paddle dusted with cornmeal. Brush the dough with 1 tablespoon of the olive oil. Top with half of the radicchio mixture, half the capers, half the olives, and half the fontina. Season with black pepper.
5. Make sure that the dough is loose from the paddle, then slide it onto the pizza stone. Bake the pizza until lightly browned, 10 to 15 minutes. Remove from the oven and repeat with the remaining dough, olive oil, and topping ingredients. Serve hot.

PIZZA WITH OYSTER MUSHROOMS, SWEET ONION, AND FONTINA CHEESE

Makes two 10-inch pizzas

Almost any type of mushroom will work with this pizza. To avoid a soggy crust, make sure that any mushrooms with a lot of moisture are cooked until liquid is reduced before being placed on the pizza.

1 recipe Pizza Dough (page 144)
3 tablespoons olive oil
2 Vidalia onions, thinly sliced
2 cloves garlic, minced
12 ounces fresh oyster mushrooms, thinly sliced
Cornmeal for dusting paddle

2 tablespoons chopped fresh thyme
4 tablespoons chopped fresh parsley
12 ounces fontina cheese, cut into ½-inch cubes
¼ cup grated Parmesan cheese
Salt and pepper

1. Prepare the pizza dough and set aside.
2. Heat 1 tablespoon of the olive oil in a large sauté pan over medium-high heat. Add the onion and garlic; sauté for 5 minutes. Stir in the mushrooms; reduce the heat to medium and continue to cook for 4 to 5 minutes, stirring occasionally. Set aside.
3. Preheat the oven with a pizza stone inside to 475°.
4. Place the pizza dough on a floured worktable. Using your fingertips press the pizza dough into a circle 10 to 12 inches in diameter and about ¼ inch thick. Transfer the dough to a wooden paddle dusted with cornmeal. Brush the dough with 1 tablespoon of the olive oil; top with half of the mushroom mixture and half of the herbs and cheeses. Season with salt and pepper.
5. Make sure that the dough is loose from the paddle, then slide the pizza onto the stone. Bake the pizza until lightly browned, about 10 to 15 minutes. Remove from the oven and repeat with the remaining dough, olive oil, and topping ingredients. Serve hot.

RATATOUILLE PIZZA

Makes two 10-inch pizzas

Classic ratatouille is a long-simmered vegetable stew, but to give this pizza texture the cooking time has been shortened. The ratatouille can be made well in advance and kept at room temperature for a few hours or refrigerated overnight.

1 recipe Pizza Dough (page 144)
3 tablespoons olive oil
2 small onions, finely diced
3 cloves garlic, minced
1 small eggplant, peeled and finely diced
2 tomatoes, peeled, seeded, and diced
1 small zucchini, finely diced
Salt and pepper
2 tablespoons chopped fresh basil

2 tablespoons chopped fresh oregano
3 tablespoon chopped fresh parsley
1 teaspoon balsamic vinegar
Cornmeal for dusting paddle
12 ounces fresh mozzarella cheese, thinly sliced
¼ cup grated Parmesan cheese

1. Prepare the pizza dough and set aside.
2. Heat 1 tablespoon of the olive oil in a large sauté pan over medium-high heat. Add the onion and garlic; sauté for 3 to 4 minutes. Add the eggplant, tomato, and zucchini; season with salt and pepper. Reduce the heat to medium-low and cook for 10 minutes, stirring occasionally. Add the fresh herbs and cook 2 minutes longer. Remove from heat and stir in the vinegar.
3. Preheat the oven with a pizza stone inside to 475°.
4. Place the pizza dough on a floured worktable. Using your fingertips press the dough into a circle 10 to 12 inches in diameter and about ¼ inch thick. Transfer the dough to a wooden paddle dusted with cornmeal. Brush the dough with 1 tablespoon of the olive oil and top with half the eggplant mixture and half the cheeses. Season with salt and pepper.
5. Make sure that the pizza is loose from the paddle, then slide it onto the stone. Bake the pizza until lightly browned, about 10 to 15 minutes. Remove from the oven and repeat with the remaining dough, olive oil, and topping ingredients. Serve hot.

PIZZA WITH GRILLED EGGPLANT, TOMATO, AND GOAT CHEESE

Makes two 10-inch pizzas

Grilled eggplant, tomato, basil, and goat cheese are a winning flavor combination. Most varieties of eggplant are similar and interchangeable in many dishes, including this one. When selecting eggplant, look for those that are firm and heavy. The skin should be dark and shiny; wrinkles or brown spots are signs of age.

1 recipe Pizza Dough (page 144)	4 tablespoons chopped fresh basil
4 tablespoons olive oil	3 tablespoons chopped fresh chives
2 cloves garlic, minced	4 ounces goat cheese, crumbled
1 small eggplant, thinly sliced	6 ounces fontina cheese, cut into
Cornmeal for dusting paddle	½-inch cubes
3 tomatoes, peeled, seeded, and diced	Salt and pepper

1. Prepare the pizza dough and set aside.
2. Heat the olive oil and garlic in a small saucepan over medium-high heat just until the garlic starts to brown. Remove from the heat and allow to stand for 1 hour. Meanwhile, prepare a charcoal grill.
3. Strain the oil and discard the garlic. Set the oil aside.
4. Brush both sides of the eggplant with 2 tablespoons of the garlic oil. Grill the eggplant over a medium-high fire until it is browned on both sides, about 2 to 3 minutes per side. Set aside.
5. Preheat the oven with a pizza stone inside to 475°.
6. Place the pizza dough on a floured worktable. Using your fingertips press the dough into a circle 10 to 12 inches in diameter and about ¼ inch thick. Transfer the dough to a wooden paddle dusted with cornmeal. Brush the dough with 1 tablespoon of the garlic oil and arrange half of the grilled eggplant slices on top. Top the eggplant with half of the tomato, herbs, and half the cheeses. Season with salt and pepper.
7. Make sure that the pizza is loose from the paddle, then slide it onto the pizza stone. Bake the pizza until lightly browned, about 10 to 15 minutes. Remove from the oven and repeat with the remaining dough, garlic oil, eggplant, and topping ingredients. Serve hot.

FIRST COURSES

LOBSTER GUMBO

Gumbo is a Cajun soup that may contain a variety of vegetables, seafood, and meats. The distinct flavor of gumbo comes from cooking the roux to a dark brown stage. Roux is a mixture of flour and oil or butter used to thicken soups and sauces. Because of the extremely high temperature of the roux, care must be taken when making it and when stirring it into the simmering stock.

LOBSTER STOCK	GUMBO
2 lobsters (1½ pounds each)	2 small onions, finely diced
2 tablespoons olive oil	1 clove garlic, minced
1 small onion, diced	1 green bell pepper, finely diced
1 carrot, diced	1 stalk celery, finely diced
1 stalk celery, diced	1 bay leaf
1 clove garlic, peeled	1 teaspoon salt
2 tablespoons chopped fresh parsley	½ teaspoon ground black pepper
1 tablespoon chopped fresh thyme	Pinch of cayenne pepper
1 tablespoon chopped fresh chervil	½ teaspoon dried thyme
1 bay leaf	½ teaspoon dried oregano
1 cup dry white wine	½ cup canola oil
6 cups water	½ cup all-purpose flour
1 teaspoon lemon juice	1 cup cooked white rice

1. *Prepare the lobsters and stock:* Steam the lobsters for 10 minutes; remove from the heat and allow to cool.
2. Remove the lobster meat from the tail and claw sections; reserve the shells. Dice the meat and set aside for the gumbo. Split the body section of the lobster in half and discard the green tomalley, the sand sac behind the eyes, and the gill tissues. Rinse the body section under cold water. Chop the body and the tail and claw shells into small pieces for the stock.
3. Heat the olive oil in a large stockpot over medium-high heat. Add the onion, carrot, celery, and garlic; sauté for 3 to 4 minutes, stirring occasionally. Add the lobster shells along with the remaining stock ingredients. Bring to a boil, reduce the heat, and slowly simmer the stock for 30 minutes.
4. Strain the stock through cheesecloth or a fine mesh strainer. Return 3 cups of the stock to the stockpot and bring to a simmer for the gumbo. Reserve any leftover stock for another use.
5. *Prepare the gumbo:* In a small bowl mix together the onion, garlic, bell pepper, and celery; set aside. In another small bowl mix together the bay leaf, salt, black pepper, cayenne, thyme, and oregano; set aside.
6. Heat the oil in a large, heavy saucepan over high heat until it begins to smoke. Slowly whisk in the flour and continue to cook until the roux is dark brown, stirring constantly. Reduce the heat to low. Using a wooden spoon, stir in the

reserved onion mixture and seasoning mixture; cook for 1 minute, stirring constantly.

7. Slowly whisk the roux mixture into the simmering lobster stock and continue to stir until well blended. Bring to a boil; reduce the heat and slowly simmer for 15 minutes.

8. Skim any fat from the surface of the stock mixture. Stir in the reserved lobster meat and the rice and continue to cook for 1 minute. Ladle the gumbo into bowls and serve hot.

FIDDLEHEAD SOUP

Serves 6

A sure sign of spring in Maine, fiddleheads are the young, tightly coiled bright green fronds of the ostrich fern. They have a mild flavor and can be used in salads, tossed with pasta, or simply sautéed in butter with a little lemon juice. To clean fiddleheads, remove the brown threads on the coils under cold running water, cutting away any brown stems. Fiddleheads will keep for 4 to 5 days refrigerated in a bowl of ice water.

2 tablespoons olive oil	¼ cup dry sherry
2 tablespoons unsalted butter	6 cups Chicken Stock (page 138)
1 small sweet onion, thinly sliced	or Vegetable Stock (page 140)
1 clove garlic, minced	or as needed
½ stalk celery, thinly sliced	1 cup heavy cream
1 pound fiddleheads, cleaned	1 teaspoon lemon juice
2 tablespoons chopped fresh chervil	Salt and pepper

1. Heat the olive oil and butter in a large saucepan over medium-high heat. Add the onion, garlic, and celery; cook for 5 minutes, stirring occasionally. Stir in the fiddleheads and chervil; cook for 2 to 3 minutes. Add the sherry and stock; gently simmer for 15 minutes. Remove 12 fiddleheads and set aside in a warm place.

2. Stir in the cream and lemon juice; cook for 2 minutes. Remove from heat and season with salt and pepper.

3. Transfer to a blender and purée until smooth, adding more stock if the soup is too thick. Check the seasoning.

4. Ladle the soup into bowls, garnish each with 2 cooked fiddleheads, and serve.

JEAN'S CRAB BISQUE

Serves 6

The spicy curry balances the sweet apple with the delicate crab to make this soup extremely appealing, especially in fall when apples are in season and crab is still plentiful. Be stingy with the curry powder so the subtle flavors are not overwhelmed.

4 tablespoons unsalted butter
1 small onion, finely diced
1 clove garlic, minced
1 small apple, peeled, cored, and
   finely diced
1 teaspoon curry powder
1 tablespoon all-purpose flour
3 cups Chicken Stock (page 138)

1 tomato, peeled, seeded, and
   chopped
½ pound crabmeat
½ cup heavy cream or milk
Salt and pepper
Few drops of Tabasco

Chopped fresh parsley for garnish

1. Heat the butter in a small saucepan over medium-high heat. Add the onion and cook for 2 to 3 minutes. Stir in the garlic and apple; cook for 1 to 2 minutes, stirring occasionally. Stir in the curry and flour; cook for 1 minute.
2. Bring the stock to a boil in a large saucepan. Slowly whisk into the curry-vegetable mixture until smooth. Bring to a boil; reduce the heat and slowly simmer for 5 minutes.
3. Stir in the tomato, crab, and cream; cook for 5 minutes over medium heat. Season with salt, pepper, and Tabasco. Ladle the bisque into bowls and serve garnished with chopped parsley.

LOBSTER GAZPACHO

Serves 6 to 8

Served very cold, this soup makes a light and refreshing first course on a hot summer day. The flavors will develop more fully if the soup is prepared in advance and refrigerated for at least 8 hours or overnight. It is essential to use fresh, ripe tomatoes; they provide a foundation of flavor for the soup.

LOBSTER STOCK
2 lobsters (1½ pounds each)
2 tablespoons olive oil
1 small onion, diced
1 carrot, diced
1 stalk celery, diced
1 clove garlic, peeled
2 tablespoons chopped fresh parsley
1 tablespoon chopped fresh thyme
1 tablespoon chopped fresh chervil
1 bay leaf
1 cup dry white wine
6 cups water
1 teaspoon lemon juice

GAZPACHO
4 tomatoes, peeled, seeded, and diced
1 cucumber, peeled, seeded, and diced
1 red bell pepper, diced
1 small onion, diced
1 small celeriac, peeled and diced
1 stalk celery, diced
1 clove garlic, minced
2 tablespoons chopped fresh chervil
1 tablespoon chopped fresh parsley
2 tablespoons chopped fresh cilantro
3 tablespoons olive oil
1 tablespoon lime juice (2 small limes)
Few drops Tabasco sauce
2 cups tomato juice
Salt and pepper
2 avocados, peeled and diced for garnish
Chopped fresh chives for garnish

1. *Prepare the lobsters and stock:* Steam the lobsters for 10 minutes; remove from the heat and allow to cool.
2. Remove the lobster meat from the tail and claw sections; reserve the shells. Dice the meat and set aside for the gazpacho. Split the body section of the lobster in half and discard the green tomalley, the sand sac behind the eyes, and the gill tissues. Rinse the body section under cold water. Chop the body and the tail and claw shells into small pieces for the stock.
3. Heat the olive oil in a large stockpot over medium-high heat. Add the onion, carrot, celery, and garlic; sauté for 3 to 4 minutes, stirring occasionally. Add the lobster shells along with the remaining stock ingredients. Bring to a boil; reduce the heat and slowly simmer the stock for 30 minutes.
4. Strain the stock through cheesecloth or a fine mesh strainer. Reserve 2 cups of the stock for the gazpacho; chill until needed.
5. *Prepare the gazpacho:* Combine all the gazpacho ingredients except the garnishes in a large bowl. Add the reserved stock and refrigerate, covered, for 8 hours. Stir in the reserved lobster meat.
6. Ladle the soup into bowls, garnish with the diced avocado and chopped chives, and serve.

LOBSTER AND SWEET CORN CHOWDER

Serves 6 to 8

This lobster and corn chowder is always received with pleasure in summer. The corn-cobs contain a sweet, milky liquid. Combining the cobs with the lobster shells in making the stock intensifies the corn flavor in the chowder. It is essential to use the freshest corn possible, preferably corn picked the same day the chowder is prepared.

LOBSTER-CORN STOCK
2 lobsters (1½ pounds each)
2 tablespoons olive oil
1 small onion, diced
1 carrot, diced
1 stalk celery, diced
1 clove garlic, peeled
4 ears of corn, kernels removed
   and set aside, cobs cut into 2-inch
   pieces
2 tablespoons chopped fresh parsley
1 bay leaf
4 cups water

LOBSTER CHOWDER
2 slices bacon, finely diced
2 cloves garlic, minced
1 onion, diced
1 stalk celery, diced
1 carrot, diced
1 tablespoon chopped fresh thyme
1 tablespoon chopped fresh chervil
   plus more for garnish
2 tablespoons chopped fresh parsley
1 russet potato, peeled and diced
1 tablespoon dry sherry
2 cups heavy cream
Salt and pepper

1. *Prepare the lobster-corn stock:* Steam the lobsters for 10 minutes; remove from heat and allow to cool.
2. Remove the lobster meat from the tail and claw sections; reserve the shells. Dice the meat and set aside for the chowder. Split the body section of the lobster in half and discard the green tomalley, the sand sac behind the eyes, and the gill tissues. Rinse the body section under cold water. Chop the body and the tail and claw shells into small pieces for the stock.
3. Heat the olive oil in a large stockpot over medium-high heat. Add the onion, carrot, celery, and garlic; sauté for 3 to 4 minutes, stirring occasionally. Add the lobster shells along with the corncob pieces, parsley, bay leaf, and water. Bring to a boil, reduce the heat, and slowly simmer the stock for 30 minutes.
4. Strain the stock through cheesecloth or a fine mesh strainer; set aside.
5. *Prepare the chowder:* Cook the bacon in a large saucepan over medium heat until golden brown and crisp. Add the garlic, onion, celery, and carrot; sauté for 4 to 5 minutes. Stir in the fresh herbs, potato, sherry, reserved lobster-corn stock, and cream. Bring to a boil; reduce the heat and simmer until the potato is cooked, about 8 to 10 minutes. Add reserved corn kernels and cook for 2 minutes longer.
6. Stir in the reserved lobster meat and season with salt and pepper. Ladle the chowder into bowls, sprinkle with chopped chervil, and serve.

CARAMELIZED ONION, TOMATO, AND PESTO SOUP

Serves 8

This soup is easy to prepare and a delicious choice for summer when tomatoes and basil are ready to harvest. Using sweet onions such as Vidalia or Walla Walla will enhance the flavor of the soup. The croutons can be prepared well in advance; store them at room temperature in an airtight container.

CROUTONS
5 tablespoons olive oil
3 cloves garlic, minced
2 cups sourdough bread
  cubes (about ½-inch thick)
Salt and pepper

SOUP
1 tablespoon olive oil
2 pounds onions, thinly sliced

1 teaspoon sugar
½ cup dry red wine
1 tablespoon chopped fresh thyme
3 cups Chicken Stock (page 138)
4 cups Beef Stock (page 139)
2 tomatoes, peeled, seeded, and diced
Salt and pepper
1 tablespoon Pesto (page 143)
Grated Parmesan cheese for garnish

1. *Prepare the croutons:* Preheat the oven to 375°. Combine the olive oil and garlic in a small saucepan and cook over medium-high heat until the garlic just starts to brown. Remove from heat and let stand at room temperature for 30 minutes.
2. Strain the garlic oil into a small bowl. Add the bread cubes and toss to coat. Transfer the bread cubes to a baking pan and bake until brown and crisp, stirring occasionally. Season with salt and pepper and set aside.
3. *Prepare the soup:* Heat the olive oil in a large saucepan over medium heat. Add the onions and sugar; sauté until the onion is well browned, about 25 to 30 minutes, stirring often.
4. Add the wine and thyme and cook for 2 minutes. Add the stocks and tomatoes and bring to a boil. Reduce the heat and slowly simmer the soup for 20 minutes. Season with salt and pepper.
5. Just before serving, stir in the pesto. Ladle the soup into bowls and serve garnished with Parmesan cheese and the reserved croutons.

ACORN SQUASH AND PEAR SOUP

Serves 6 to 8

This smooth and slightly sweet soup is especially good on cold winter days. Other varieties such as butternut, delicata, or hubbard squash can be successfully substituted for the acorn. Choose winter squash that have hard, thick shells and feel heavy for their size. If Comice pears are not available, other winter pears such as Bosc or Anjou can be used.

1 acorn squash (about 3 pounds)	1 russet potato, peeled and diced
2 tablespoons unsalted butter	5 cups Chicken Stock (page 138)
2 shallots, finely diced	1 cup heavy cream or milk
1 stalk celery, diced	2 tablespoons pear liqueur
1 teaspoon curry powder	Salt and pepper
1 teaspoon chopped fresh rosemary	
2 Comice pears, peeled, cored, and sliced	Chopped fresh parsley for garnish

1. Preheat the oven to 350°. Line a baking pan with parchment paper or aluminum foil; if using foil, grease it.
2. Cut the squash in half; scoop out and discard the seeds. Place the squash cut side down on the prepared pan. Bake until the squash is soft, about 40 to 50 minutes. Remove from the oven and allow to cool. Scoop out the squash flesh and set aside.
3. Heat the butter in a large saucepan over medium-high heat. Add the shallot and celery; cook for 1 minute. Stir in the curry powder and rosemary; continue to cook for 1 minute. Stir in the pear, potato, stock, cream, pear liqueur, and reserved squash. Bring to a boil, reduce the heat, and gently simmer for 20 minutes.
4. Remove the soup from the heat and season with salt and pepper. Transfer to a blender and purée until smooth. Return to the saucepan and cook over low heat for 1 minute.
5. Check the seasoning. Ladle the soup into bowls and serve garnished with chopped parsley.

MUSSEL, SAFFRON, AND CELERIAC SOUP

Serves 6

Satisfying and easy to prepare, this light chowder is enhanced by the sweetness and delicacy of celeriac. After peeling and cutting the celeriac, immediately place it in acidulated water (water with a teaspoon of lemon juice) to keep it white. The tangle of threads found on the mussel shells is the "beard," used by the mussel to attach itself to ropes and rocks. Pull off and discard the beard and scrub the mussels under cold running water.

MUSSEL BROTH
2 tablespoons unsalted butter
1 small onion, diced
1 carrot, diced
1 stalk celery, diced
1 clove garlic, minced
1 tablespoon chopped fresh parsley
1 bay leaf
½ cup dry white wine
2 cups Chicken Stock (page 138)
2 pounds mussels, debearded and
   scrubbed

SOUP
2 tablespoons unsalted butter
3 shallots, finely diced
1 clove garlic, minced
1 medium celeriac (about 1 pound),
   peeled and finely diced
Pinch of saffron
1 teaspoon chopped fresh thyme
1 tablespoon chopped fresh dill
2 cups heavy cream or milk
Salt and pepper

1. *Prepare the mussels and broth:* Heat the butter in a large saucepan over medium heat. Add the onion, carrot, celery, and garlic; sauté for 3 to 4 minutes. Add the parsley, bay leaf, wine, stock, and mussels. Cover and cook until the mussels open, about 4 to 5 minutes, shaking the pan occasionally. Remove from heat and allow to cool.

2. Remove the mussels from the pan and set aside. Discard any unopened mussels. Strain the broth through cheesecloth or a fine mesh strainer. You should have about 3 cups of broth.

3. Remove the mussels from their shells and set aside. Discard the shells.

4. *Prepare the soup:* Heat the butter in a large saucepan over medium heat. Add the shallot and garlic; sauté for 2 minutes. Add the celeriac; reduce the heat to low and cook for 5 minutes, stirring occasionally. Stir in the saffron, thyme, dill, and reserved mussel broth. Bring to a simmer and cook for 2 minutes.

5. Stir in the cream and cook for 2 minutes longer. Add the reserved mussels and cook for 1 minute. Season with salt and pepper. Ladle the soup into bowls and serve.

POTATO, LEEK, AND FONTINA SOUP

Serves 6 to 8

This is an ideal soup for the cool autumn months. It is the starch content of russet potatoes that gives this soup body and a smooth consistency; however, other potatoes can be substituted. Select potatoes that are smooth and firm with no sprouts or green spots.

1 tablespoon olive oil
3 leeks, white part only, finely diced
2 cloves garlic, minced
2 shallots, finely diced
2 tablespoons dry sherry
2½ pounds russet potatoes,
   peeled and diced

5 cups Chicken Stock (page 138)
1 cup heavy cream or milk
Salt and white pepper
5 ounces fontina cheese, cut into
   small cubes
2 tablespoons chopped fresh chervil
2 tablespoons chopped fresh chives

1. Heat the olive oil in a large saucepan over medium-high heat. Add the leeks, garlic, and shallots; cook for 4 to 5 minutes, stirring occasionally. Add the sherry and cook for 2 minutes. Add the potatoes and stock; bring to a boil, reduce the heat, and slowly simmer for 15 minutes. Add the cream, season with salt and pepper, and continue to cook until the potato is soft, about 5 minutes.
2. Remove the soup from the heat and stir in the cheese. Transfer the soup to a blender and purée until smooth. Check the seasoning.
3. Ladle the soup into bowls and serve garnished with the chervil and chives.

ROASTED RED PEPPER, GARLIC, AND FENNEL SOUP WITH MAINE CRAB

Serves 6 to 8

Especially good when tomatoes are at their peak, the anise flavor of the fennel is a nice match to the sweetness of the crab. The strong garlic flavor, which mellows when roasted, imparts a mild, nutty flavor to the soup. The roasted bell peppers and garlic can be prepared well in advance and refrigerated until needed. Squeeze out the soft garlic from its bulb before storing in the refrigerator; it is much harder to remove when chilled. Grilling the bell peppers over charcoal gives the soup a smoky flavor. The tomatoes may also be grilled for a more intense flavor.

1 bulb garlic
3 tablespoons olive oil
5 red bell peppers
2 leeks, white part only, finely diced
2 bulbs fennel, trimmed and sliced
5 tomatoes, peeled, seeded, and diced
2 tablespoons chopped fresh chervil
7 cups Chicken Stock (page 138)

1 tablespoon Pernod or other
    anise-flavored liqueur
Salt and pepper
12 ounces crabmeat
1 teaspoon lemon juice

Chopped fresh chives for garnish

1. Preheat the oven to 300°. Rub the garlic with 1 tablespoon of the olive oil and place in a small roasting pan. Cover with aluminum foil and bake for 1 hour.

2. Meanwhile, place the bell peppers over a charcoal fire or gas flame or under the broiler. Roast until the skin is uniformly charred, turning the peppers as needed. Place the peppers in a plastic bag, seal tightly, and allow to steam for 30 minutes. Remove the peppers from the bag, peel away the skin, cut the peppers in half, and discard the seeds and stems. Finely dice the peppers and set aside.

3. Remove the garlic from the oven and allow to cool for 30 minutes. Cut a ½-inch slice off the top of the bulb with a serrated knife and squeeze out the soft garlic. Set aside.

4. Heat the remaining 2 tablespoons olive oil in a large saucepan over medium-high heat. Add the leek and fennel; cook for 3 to 4 minutes, stirring often. Reduce the heat to medium and add the tomato and chervil; continue to cook for 2 to 3 minutes. Stir in the stock, Pernod, and the roasted peppers and garlic; bring to a boil, reduce the heat, and gently simmer for 10 minutes.

5. Remove the soup from the heat; transfer to a blender and purée until smooth. Return the soup to the saucepan and season with salt and pepper. Stir in the crabmeat and lemon juice; warm for 1 minute over medium heat. Ladle into bowls and serve garnished with chives.

COCONUT CARROT SOUP

Serves 8 to 10

This brightly colored, delicately seasoned soup can be served any time of the year. The coconut milk gives the soup sweetness and body.

2 tablespoons unsalted butter
2 teaspoons chopped fresh ginger
2 shallots, finely diced
1 stalk celery, finely diced
1 jalapeño pepper, finely diced
1 clove garlic, minced
2 pounds carrots, peeled and diced
1 teaspoon ground cumin
1 teaspoon ground coriander
½ teaspoon ground turmeric
Pinch of ground cinnamon

½ teaspoon paprika
6 cups Chicken Stock (page 138)
  or as needed
2 cups unsweetened coconut milk
Salt and pepper
½ cup sliced almonds (about 3
  ounces), toasted
1 tablespoon lime juice

Chopped fresh cilantro for garnish

1. Heat the butter in a large saucepan over medium-high heat. Add the ginger, shallot, celery, jalapeño, and garlic; cook for 2 minutes. Add the carrot, cumin, coriander, turmeric, cinnamon, paprika, and ½ cup of the stock. Reduce the heat to medium-low, cover, and continue to cook for 3 to 4 minutes, stirring occasionally.
2. Stir in the remaining 5½ cups stock and the coconut milk. Season with salt and pepper. Bring to a boil; reduce heat and slowly simmer until the carrots are soft, about 15 to 20 minutes.
3. Remove the soup from the heat and stir in the almonds and lime juice. Transfer to a blender and purée until smooth, adding more stock if the soup is too thick. Check the seasoning.
4. Ladle the soup into bowls and serve garnished with chopped cilantro.

Wild mushrooms from Pam Pace

In late summer, our friend Pam Pace begins appearing at the back door carrying baskets filled with freshly picked wild mushrooms. An experienced and dedicated mycologist, Pam at an early age learned the secrets of wild mushrooms from her mother. The passion she feels and the pleasure she derives from mushroom gathering are evident when she enters our kitchen, proudly displaying her harvest of chanterelles, cepes, shaggy manes, honeys, or suillus.

Pam believes wild mushrooms have much more flavor and better texture than the cultivated varieties. They have a rich, earthy fragrance and a firm, meaty texture, needing little more than a brief sauté in olive oil to bring to mind a walk in the woods. She shares her knowledge generously with other enthusiasts, leading mushroom hunts and explaining distinctive characteristics, but understandably, she keeps certain spots secret.

The fruits of Pam's labors can be tasted in a variety of dishes at the Inn: tossed with our homemade pasta, featured in the risotto, marinated and grilled over hickory, or delicately roasted and used to garnish fish, chicken, and meats.

Since the early 1950s, Pam has spent half of each year in Deer Isle with her husband, Stephen, a well-known artist who finds inspiration in the island's beauty and simplicity. We, at the Inn, find inspiration in Pam's enthusiasm and expertise and the efforts she makes to provide us with these rare treats.

—*Jean and Dud Hendrick*

RISOTTO WITH MAINE LOBSTER
AND CHANTERELLE MUSHROOMS

Serves 4

The combination of lobster and chanterelle mushrooms creates a colorful risotto with a delightful, rich flavor. Chanterelle mushrooms grow wild on Deer Isle; they are golden in color and have a buttery flavor, superb when matched with lobster. If chanterelle mushrooms are not available, you can substitute fresh oyster, porcini, or portabello mushrooms.

LOBSTER STOCK
2 lobsters (1½ pounds each)
2 tablespoons olive oil
1 small onion, diced
1 carrot, diced
1 stalk celery, diced
1 clove garlic, peeled
2 tablespoons chopped fresh parsley
1 tablespoon chopped fresh thyme
1 tablespoon chopped fresh chervil
1 bay leaf
1 cup dry white wine
6 cups water
1 tablespoon lemon juice

MUSHROOMS
2 tablespoons unsalted butter
2 cups fresh chanterelle mushrooms
   (4 to 5 ounces), cleaned and sliced
Salt and pepper

RISOTTO
2 tablespoons olive oil
2 tablespoons unsalted butter
2 shallots, finely diced
2 cloves garlic, minced
1 small leek, white part only, finely
   diced
1 cup Arborio rice
1 cup dry white wine
1 tomato, peeled, seeded, and diced
1 tablespoon chopped fresh parsley
1 tablespoon chopped fresh chervil
Salt and pepper

1. *Prepare the lobsters and stock:* Steam the lobsters for 10 minutes; remove from the heat and allow to cool.
2. Remove the lobster meat from the tail and claw sections; reserve the shells. Dice the meat and set aside for the risotto. Split the body section of the lobster in half and discard the green tomalley, the sand sac behind the eyes, and the gill tissues. Rinse the body section under cold water. Chop the body and the tail and claw shells into small pieces for the stock.
3. Heat the olive oil in a large stockpot over medium-high heat. Add the onion, carrot, celery, and garlic; sauté for 3 to 4 minutes, stirring occasionally. Add the lobster shells along with the remaining stock ingredients. Bring to a boil, reduce the heat, and slowly simmer the stock for 30 minutes.
4. Strain the stock through cheesecloth or a fine mesh strainer. Return 4½ cups of

the stock to the stockpot and bring to a simmer for the risotto. Reserve any left-over stock for another use.

5. *Prepare the mushrooms:* Heat the butter in a sauté pan over medium heat. Add the mushrooms, season with salt and pepper, and cook for 3 to 4 minutes, stirring occasionally. Set aside.

6. *Prepare the risotto:* Maintain the reserved 4½ cups lobster stock at a simmer throughout the risotto preparation. Heat the olive oil and butter in a large skillet over medium-high heat. Add the shallot, garlic, and leek; cook for 2 minutes. Add the rice. Using a wooden spoon, stir to coat the rice with the oil and butter. Add the wine and cook until most of the wine is absorbed, about 2 minutes, stirring constantly to prevent sticking.

7. Start adding enough stock to barely cover the rice, about 1 cup. Adjust the heat to maintain the risotto at a gentle simmer. As the rice absorbs the stock, add more stock to keep the level of the liquid just above the rice, stirring constantly.

8. After approximately 15 minutes, the rice should be tender but still firm. Stir in the reserved mushrooms, lobster meat, tomato, and herbs. Season with salt and pepper and cook for 2 minutes. Remove from heat and serve immediately.

ABOUT RISOTTO

A good-quality stock is essential for making risotto. It should match the main ingredient of the risotto: lamb or beef stock for meats, fish stock for seafood, and chicken or duck stock for poultry. For risotto that is made with only vegetables, use a flavorful vegetable or wild mushroom stock. Remember when making stock to use only fresh ingredients.

It is important to keep the stock simmering while you add it to the rice, and to keep the risotto at an even simmer to ensure the correct rate of evaporation of the stock. If the temperature of the risotto is too high, the stock will evaporate too quickly and the rice may stick to the pan and burn. If the temperature is too low, the stock will take longer to be absorbed and the texture of the risotto will be soft and mushy instead of firm and creamy.

RISOTTO WITH DRIED AND FRESH MUSHROOMS, LEEKS, AND FONTINA CHEESE

Serves 6

The combination of dried and fresh mushrooms gives this dish an earthy, woodsy flavor.

6 cups Chicken Stock (page 138)
½ ounce dried porcini mushrooms
3 tablespoons olive oil
8 ounces fresh wild mushrooms (any combination of chanterelle, shiitake, morel, or portabello), finely diced
Salt and pepper
2 tablespoons unsalted butter
1 leek, white part only, thinly sliced

2 cloves garlic, minced
1½ cups Arborio rice
1 cup dry white wine
1 tablespoon chopped fresh oregano
1 tablespoon chopped fresh parsley
1 tablespoon chopped fresh chives
4 ounces fontina cheese, cut into small pieces
¼ cup grated Parmesan cheese

1. Bring 1 cup of the stock to a boil in a small saucepan. Add the dried mushrooms, remove from the heat, and allow to stand for 1 hour.
2. Strain the stock into a large saucepan and reserve the mushrooms. Return the stock to the saucepan. Add the remaining 5 cups stock to the saucepan and bring to a simmer.
3. Meanwhile, chop the soaked mushrooms. Heat 1 tablespoon of the olive oil in a sauté pan over medium-high heat. Add the dried and fresh mushrooms and sauté until the mushrooms are soft, about 5 minutes, stirring often. Season with salt and pepper and set aside.
4. *Prepare the risotto:* Maintain the stock at a simmer throughout the risotto preparation. Heat the remaining 2 tablespoons olive oil and the butter in a large skillet. Add the leek and garlic; sauté for 1 minute. Add the rice. Using a wooden spoon, stir to coat the rice with the olive oil and butter. Add the wine and cook until most of the wine is absorbed, about 1 to 2 minutes, stirring constantly to prevent sticking.
5. Start adding enough stock to barely cover the rice, about 1 cup. Adjust the heat to maintain the risotto at a gentle simmer. As the rice absorbs the stock, add more stock to keep the level of the liquid just above the rice, stirring constantly.
6. After approximately 15 minutes, the rice should be tender but still firm. Stir in the herbs and sautéed mushrooms; cook for 2 minutes. Remove from heat and stir in the cheeses. Season with salt and pepper. Serve immediately.

RISOTTO WITH ARUGULA, TOMATO, AND PINE NUTS

Serves 6

In addition to a fine first course, this risotto makes a satisfying lunch with a salad of fresh garden greens and slices of French or Italian bread. The peppery flavor of the arugula balances the richness of the cheeses in the risotto. The vegetables, herbs, and cheeses are added during the final preparation to ensure that they do not overcook and lose their flavor in the rice.

6 cups Chicken Stock (page 138)
2 tablespoons olive oil
2 tablespoons unsalted butter
2 cloves garlic, minced
3 shallots, finely diced
3 ounces fresh shiitake mushrooms, finely diced
1½ cups Arborio rice
1 cup dry white wine
2 tomatoes, peeled, seeded, and chopped

1 bunch (about 4 ounces) arugula, washed, dried, and chopped
¼ cup pine nuts, toasted
2 tablespoons chopped fresh basil
1 tablespoon chopped fresh thyme
2 tablespoons chopped fresh parsley
2 tablespoons grated Parmesan cheese
3 ounces fresh mozzarella cheese, thinly sliced
Salt and pepper

1. Bring the stock to a slow simmer in a medium saucepan and maintain a simmer throughout the risotto preparation.
2. Heat the oil and butter in a large skillet over medium-high heat. Add the garlic, shallots, and mushrooms; sauté for 1 to 2 minutes. Add the rice. Using a wooden spoon, stir to coat the rice with the oil and butter. Add the wine and cook until most of the wine is absorbed, about 1 to 2 minutes, stirring constantly to prevent sticking.
3. Start adding enough stock to barely cover the rice, about 1 cup. Adjust the heat to maintain the risotto at a gentle simmer. As the rice absorbs the stock, add more stock to keep the level of the liquid just above the rice, stirring constantly.
4. After approximately 15 minutes, the rice should be tender but still firm. Stir in the tomato, arugula, pine nuts, and herbs; cook for 2 minutes. Remove from heat and stir in the cheeses. Season with salt and pepper and serve immediately.

RISOTTO WITH BRAISED LAMB AND ROSEMARY

Serves 6

For convenience, the lamb and stock can be prepared a few hours in advance or the day before. Cover and refrigerate until needed.

LAMB AND STOCK	RISOTTO
2 lamb shanks, trimmed of fat	2 tablespoons olive oil
Salt and pepper	2 tablespoons unsalted butter
1 tablespoon olive oil	3 shallots, finely diced
1 small onion, finely diced	2 cloves garlic, minced
1 stalk celery, finely diced	1½ cups Arborio rice
1 carrot, finely diced	1 cup dry white wine
1 clove garlic, minced	1 tablespoon chopped fresh rosemary
1 tablespoon chopped fresh parsley	2 tablespoons chopped fresh parsley
1 tomato, peeled, seeded, and diced	2 teaspoons chopped fresh thyme
1 bay leaf	¼ cup grated Parmesan cheese
10–12 cups cold water	Salt and pepper

1. *Prepare the lamb and stock:* Season the lamb shanks with salt and pepper. Heat the olive oil in a large saucepan over medium heat. Add the lamb shanks and cook for 10 to 15 minutes, turning to brown all sides.

2. Remove the shanks and set aside. Remove and discard all but 1 tablespoon of fat in the saucepan. To the saucepan add the onion, celery, carrot, and garlic; sauté for 2 to 3 minutes. Return the shanks to the pan along with the parsley, tomato, and bay leaf. Cover with the cold water; bring to a boil, reduce the heat, and simmer gently for 2 hours.

3. Remove the shanks from the pan and set aside to cool. Strain the stock and discard the vegetables. Skim off any fat from the surface of the stock. Return 6 cups of the stock to the pan and bring to a simmer for the risotto. Reserve the remaining stock for another use.

4. Once the shanks have cooled, remove the meat from the bones and chop into small pieces. Set aside.

5. *Prepare the risotto:* Maintain the reserved 6 cups stock at a slow simmer throughout the risotto preparation. Heat the olive oil and butter in a large skillet over medium-high heat. Add the shallots and garlic; sauté for 1 minute. Add the rice. Using a wooden spoon, stir the rice until well coated with the butter and oil. Add the wine and cook until most of the wine is absorbed, about 1 to 2 minutes, stirring constantly to prevent sticking.

6. Start adding enough stock to barely cover the rice, about 1 cup. Adjust the heat to maintain the risotto at a gentle simmer. As the rice absorbs the stock, add more stock to keep the level of the liquid just above the rice, stirring constantly.

7. After approximately 15 minutes, the rice should be tender but still firm. Stir in the herbs and lamb meat; cook for 2 minutes. Remove from heat and stir in the cheese. Season with salt and pepper and serve immediately.

RISOTTO WITH DUCK CONFIT

Serves 6

The richness of the duck makes this risotto a good choice for a hearty midwinter dinner. A whole roasted duck—skinned, boned, and the meat cut into small pieces—can be substituted for the duck confit. Chicken will also work well if duck is not available. Use cooked chicken thigh meat instead of breast meat for a more intense flavor. Once you become familiar with the basic technique for preparing risotto, you will discover that the potential ingredients for making it are endless. Risotto is also an ideal way to use leftover vegetables, meats, and seafood.

6 cups Chicken Stock (page 138)
   or duck stock
2 tablespoons olive oil
2 tablespoons unsalted butter
2 cloves garlic, minced
3 shallots, finely diced
2 teaspoons chopped fresh ginger
1½ cups Arborio rice
1 cup dry white wine

3 leg-thighs Duck Confit (page 106),
   boned and meat cut into small
   pieces
2 tablespoons chopped fresh parsley
2 tablespoons chopped fresh cilantro
2 ounces fontina cheese, cut into
   small pieces
Salt and pepper

1. Bring the stock to a simmer in a medium saucepan and maintain a simmer throughout the preparation of the risotto.
2. Heat the olive oil and butter in a large skillet over medium-high heat. Add the garlic, shallots, and ginger; sauté for 1 to 2 minutes. Add the rice. Using a wooden spoon, stir to coat the rice with the oil and butter. Add the wine and cook until most of the wine is absorbed, about 1 to 2 minutes, stirring constantly to prevent sticking.
3. Start adding enough stock to barely cover the rice, about 1 cup. Adjust the heat to maintain the risotto at a gentle simmer. As the rice absorbs the stock, add more stock to keep the level of the liquid just above the rice, stirring constantly.
4. After approximately 15 minutes, the rice should be tender but still firm. Stir in the duck and fresh herbs and cook for 1 minute. Remove from heat and stir in the cheese. Season with salt and pepper and serve immediately.

RAVIOLI WITH CHICKEN, RICOTTA, SWISS CHARD, AND CHICKEN REDUCTION

Serves 8

CHICKEN AND STOCK
1 tablespoon olive oil
1 small onion, finely diced
1 carrot, finely diced
1 stalk celery, finely diced
3 chicken thighs
1 bay leaf
1 sprig fresh parsley
1 sprig fresh thyme
Salt and pepper

FILLING
1 tablespoon olive oil
2 cloves garlic, minced
2 shallots, minced

6 ounces Swiss chard, stems removed,
  leaves washed, dried, and chopped
6 tablespoons ricotta cheese
2 tablespoons chopped fresh basil
2 tablespoons chopped fresh parsley
Salt and pepper

RAVIOLI
1 recipe Basic Pasta Dough (page 143)
Flour for dusting
Cornmeal for dusting
4 tablespoons unsalted butter, softened

Chopped fresh chives for garnish
Toasted pine nuts for garnish

1. *Prepare the chicken and reduction:* Heat the olive oil in a saucepan over medium-high heat. Add the onion, carrot, and celery; sauté for 4 to 5 minutes. Add the chicken, bay leaf, parsley, and thyme. Cover with cold water and bring to a boil; reduce the heat and slowly simmer for 1 hour.
2. Remove the chicken and allow to cool. Strain the stock and return it to the pan. Skim the surface of any fat, then slowly simmer the stock until it is reduced to ¼ cup. Remove the reduction from the heat, season with salt and pepper, and set aside.
3. Remove the meat from the chicken thighs. Finely dice the meat, then set aside for the filling.
4. *Prepare the filling:* Heat the olive oil in a large skillet over medium-high heat. Add the garlic and cook just until it starts to brown. Add the shallots and chard; reduce the heat to medium-low and cook until chard wilts, about 2 to 3 minutes, stirring often. Remove from heat, transfer to a bowl, and allow to cool.
5. Stir the reserved chicken, the ricotta, and herbs into the chard mixture; mix until well blended. Season with salt and pepper and set aside.
6. *Prepare the ravioli:* Prepare the Basic Pasta Dough. Roll the dough through a pasta machine, starting with the widest setting and working down to the next-to-last setting, dusting with flour when necessary to prevent sticking. Cut the dough into 10- to 12-inch lengths and dust lightly with flour.
7. Place the sheets on a floured worktable. Fold one sheet in half lengthwise. Unfold the sheet and use the crease as a guide for the filling. Place 2 teaspoons of the filling just below the crease and leave 2 inches between each mound of filling.

8. Using a brush or spray bottle, lightly moisten the dough around each mound of filling with water. Fold the top half of the dough over the filling, lining it up with the bottom of the dough.

9. Press between each ravioli to remove any air and form a seal. Cut out the ravioli with a ravioli cutter or 3-inch cookie cutter. Using your thumb and first finger, press around the edge of each ravioli to seal it tightly. Transfer the ravioli to a baking pan lined with a kitchen towel dusted with cornmeal. Repeat with the remaining sheets of dough.

10. Cook the ravioli in a large pot of salted boiling water for 3 to 4 minutes.

11. Meanwhile, warm the chicken reduction over low heat and slowly whisk in the butter; do not allow to boil.

12. Remove the ravioli from the pot and divide among 8 serving plates. Drizzle 1 to 2 tablespoons of the chicken reduction over the ravioli. Serve garnished with chives and pine nuts.

ABOUT RAVIOLI

When rolling out the pasta dough to make ravioli, work with only a few sheets at a time. If the dough starts to dry out, it will be difficult to work with. Work quickly and use as little flour as possible. However, the weather does play a role in the moisture content of the dough. On a humid day it may be necessary to use more flour when rolling and shaping the dough. On a dry day it may be necessary to add more oil or water when making the dough and to use less flour when rolling and shaping it. Once you become familiar with making pasta, you will be able to feel with your hands when the pasta is the right consistency.

Before cutting ravioli make sure that the mound of filling is in the center of each ravioli. This will ensure a better seal and prevent the filling from leaking out while cooking. Ravioli can be cut with a ravioli cutter or a pastry cutter and cut into squares or rectangles. The ravioli can be prepared in advance, then covered with a kitchen towel dusted with flour and stored in the refrigerator for short periods. To store ravioli in the freezer, place them in a single layer on baking pans in the freezer until they are hard (about 1 hour), then transfer them to plastic freezer bags.

THREE-CHEESE RAVIOLI WITH SAGE BUTTER

Serves 8

FILLING
8 ounces ricotta cheese
4 ounces goat cheese, softened
½ cup grated Parmesan cheese
2 tablespoons bread crumbs
Salt and pepper

SAGE BUTTER
5 ounces unsalted butter
2 tablespoons chopped fresh sage
1 clove garlic, minced

RAVIOLI
1 recipe Basic Pasta Dough (page 143)
Flour for dusting
Cornmeal for dusting
1 tablespoon olive oil
2 tomatoes, peeled, seeded, and finely diced

Chopped fresh chives for garnish

1. *Prepare the filling:* Stir together the cheeses and bread crumbs in a bowl until well blended. Season with salt and pepper and set aside.
2. *Prepare the sage butter:* Heat the butter, sage, and garlic in a small saucepan over medium-low heat. Allow the mixture to sizzle for about 1 minute (do not allow it to burn), then strain it into a bowl and set aside in a warm place.
3. *Prepare the ravioli:* Prepare the Basic Pasta Dough. Roll the dough through a pasta machine, starting with the widest setting and working down to the next-to-last setting, dusting with flour when necessary to prevent sticking. Cut the dough into 10- to 12-inch lengths and dust lightly with flour.
4. Place the sheets on a floured worktable. Fold one sheet in half lengthwise. Unfold the sheet and use the crease as a guide for the filling. Place 2 teaspoons of the filling just below the crease and leave 2 inches between each mound of filling.
5. Using a brush or spray bottle, lightly moisten the dough around each mound of filling with water. Fold the top half of the dough over the filling, lining it up with the bottom of the dough.
6. Press between each ravioli to remove any air and form a seal. Cut out the ravioli with a ravioli cutter or 3-inch cookie cutter. Using your thumb and first finger, press around the edge of each ravioli to seal it tightly. Transfer the ravioli to a baking pan lined with a kitchen towel dusted with cornmeal. Repeat with the remaining sheets of dough.
7. Cook the ravioli in a large pot of salted boiling water for 3 to 4 minutes.
8. Meanwhile, in a small sauté pan heat the olive oil over medium-high heat. Add the tomato and heat for 1 minute.
9. Place a portion of the tomato mixture in the center of each serving plate. Surround it with the cooked ravioli and drizzle with the sage butter. Garnish with chopped chives and serve immediately.

PUMPKIN RAVIOLI WITH SPINACH AND GOAT CHEESE

Serves 6

PASTA
2 cups all-purpose flour or as needed
2 eggs
1 tablespoon water or as needed
1 tablespoon olive oil
4 tablespoons pumpkin purée
½ teaspoon salt

FILLING
12 ounces spinach, stems removed,
  leaves washed and dried
4 ounces goat cheese, crumbled
6 ounces ricotta cheese
¼ cup grated Parmesan cheese
2 tablespoons chopped fresh parsley
Pinch of ground nutmeg
Salt and pepper

CARAMELIZED ONION
4 tablespoons unsalted butter
6 onions, finely diced
1 teaspoon sugar

SAUCE
1 cup Chicken Stock (page 138)
1 shallot, minced
¾ cup heavy cream
1 tablespoon chopped fresh savory
6 tablespoons unsalted butter, softened

RAVIOLI
Flour for dusting
Cornmeal for dusting

1. *Prepare the pasta:* Combine all the pasta ingredients in a food processor and process until dough forms, adding more water or flour if the dough is too dry or moist. Transfer the dough to a floured worktable and knead until smooth and firm. Wrap in a kitchen towel and allow to rest at room temperature for 1 hour before rolling and cutting.

2. *Prepare the filling:* Steam or boil the spinach until wilted. Allow to cool, then squeeze out as much moisture as possible and finely chop. Place the spinach in a bowl and stir in the remaining filling ingredients; mix until thoroughly combined. Set aside.

3. *Prepare the caramelized onion:* Heat the butter in a large skillet over medium-high heat. Add the onion and sugar; cook until well browned, about 20 to 30 minutes, stirring occasionally. Set aside in a warm place.

4. *Prepare the sauce:* Place the stock and shallot in a small saucepan over medium-high heat; cook until reduced to ½ cup. Add the cream and reduce to ¼ cup. Turn the heat to low, stir in the savory, then whisk in the butter a few pieces at a time; do not allow to boil. Set aside in a warm place.

5. *Prepare the ravioli:* Roll the prepared dough through a pasta machine, starting with the widest setting and working down to the next-to-last setting, dusting with flour when necessary to prevent sticking.

6. Cut the dough into 12-inch lengths and dust lightly with flour.

7. Place the sheets on a floured worktable. Fold one sheet in half lengthwise. Unfold the sheet and use the crease as a guide for the filling. Place 2 teaspoons of the filling just below the crease, and leave 2 inches between each mound of filling.
8. Using a brush or spray bottle, lightly moisten the dough around each mound of filling with water. Fold the top half of the dough over the filling, lining it up with the bottom of the dough.
9. Press between each ravioli to remove any air and form a seal. Cut out the ravioli with a ravioli cutter or 3-inch cookie cutter. Using your thumb and first finger, press around the edge of each ravioli to seal it tightly. Transfer the ravioli to a baking pan lined with a kitchen towel dusted with cornmeal. Repeat with the remaining sheets of dough.
10. Cook the ravioli in a large pot of salted boiling water for 3 to 4 minutes.
11. Place a portion of the caramelized onion in the center of each serving plate. Arrange the ravioli around the onion and pour a little of the sauce over the ravioli. Serve immediately.

ABOUT PASTA

Allowing the pasta dough to rest for 1 hour between the kneading and rolling relaxes the gluten in the flour and makes the dough soft and easy to work with. The dough can be prepared several hours in advance and wrapped in a kitchen towel until needed, or it can be made the day before, enclosed in plastic wrap, and refrigerated. Chilled dough should be brought to room temperature for about 1 hour before it is rolled and cut. This will make the dough more pliable and easy to work with.

Always cook pasta in a large pot of salted boiling water. The cooking time varies depending on the weather, the type of flour used in the dough, the shape of the noodles, and whether the pasta is dried or fresh. Fresh pasta cooks quickly, anywhere from 30 seconds to 2 minutes depending on the thickness of the noodles. Dried pasta takes longer, usually 6 to 12 minutes depending on the noodle. Pasta made with all-purpose flour takes considerably less time to cook than pasta made with semolina flour. Always taste for doneness; cooked pasta should be *al dente* or slightly firm to the bite.

SPAGHETTI WITH MAINE CRAB AND PROSCIUTTO

Serves 6

1 recipe Basic Pasta Dough (page 143)
2 tablespoons unsalted butter
1 shallot, finely diced
1 carrot, finely diced
1 stalk celery, finely diced
1 clove garlic, minced
2 ounces prosciutto, finely diced
½ pound fresh crabmeat
1 tablespoon chopped fresh chervil

2 tablespoons chopped fresh parsley
2 tablespoons chopped fresh chives
1 cup Chicken Stock (page 138)
1 cup heavy cream
Salt and pepper
1 teaspoon lemon juice
Flour for dusting

¼ cup grated Parmesan cheese

1. Prepare the Basic Pasta Dough and set aside.
2. Heat the butter in a large sauté pan over medium-high heat. Add the shallot, carrot, celery, and garlic. Cook until the vegetables are soft, about 3 to 4 minutes. Add the prosciutto, crab, herbs, stock, and cream; cook for 1 minute. Remove from heat and season with salt, pepper, and lemon juice. Set aside in a warm place.
3. Roll the pasta dough through a pasta machine, starting with the widest setting and working down to the next-to-last setting, dusting with flour when necessary to prevent sticking.
4. Cut the dough into 10- to 12-inch lengths. Dust lightly with flour and run through the spaghetti cutter of the pasta machine. Place the pasta on a pasta rack or a baking pan lined with a towel dusted with cornmeal.
5. Cook the pasta in salted boiling water for 1 to 2 minutes, until *al dente* or firm to the bite. Drain the pasta and toss with the crab mixture. Divide among 6 serving plates, sprinkle with the Parmesan cheese, and serve immediately.

SPINACH TAGLIATELLE WITH TOMATO, ARUGULA, AND PARMESAN CHEESE

Serves 6

SPINACH TAGLIATELLE

1 cup unbleached all-purpose
  flour or as needed
1 cup semolina flour
1 teaspoon salt
8 ounces spinach, steamed, squeezed
  of excess liquid, and chopped
3 eggs, beaten
1 tablespoon olive oil
1 tablespoon water or as needed
All-purpose flour for dusting
Cornmeal for dusting

SAUCE

2 tablespoons olive oil
3 cloves garlic, minced
3 shallots, finely diced
4 tomatoes, peeled, seeded, and finely
  chopped
3 tablespoons chopped fresh parsley
2 bunches arugula (4 ounces each),
  washed, dried, and chopped
Salt and pepper

⅓ cup grated Parmesan cheese

1. *Prepare the tagliatelle:* Combine the flours and salt in a bowl and make a well in the center. Add the spinach, eggs, oil, and water to the well and beat them together with a fork. Begin to slowly incorporate the flour until the mixture starts to come together and forms a sticky mass of dough. Press into a ball with your hands. (If using a food processor, combine all the tagliatelle ingredients in the processor and process until dough forms, adding more water or flour if the dough is too dry or moist.)

2. Transfer the dough to a floured worktable and knead it until smooth and firm, about 10 minutes. More flour or water may be needed depending on the moisture content of the dough. Wrap the dough in a kitchen towel or plastic wrap and allow to rest for 1 hour at room temperature.

3. Roll the dough through a pasta machine, starting with the widest setting and working down to the next-to-last setting, dusting with flour when necessary to prevent sticking.

4. Cut the dough into 10- to 12-inch lengths and dust lightly with flour.

5. Run the dough through the tagliatelle cutter of the pasta machine, or cut the noodles by hand to a ¼-inch width. Place the pasta on a baking pan lined with a kitchen towel dusted with cornmeal, or hang on a pasta rack.

6. Cook the pasta in salted boiling water for 1 to 2 minutes, until *al dente* or slightly firm to the bite.

7. *Prepare the sauce:* Heat the olive oil in a large sauté pan over medium-high heat. Add the garlic and shallots; sauté for 1 minute. Add the tomatoes, parsley, and arugula; cook just until heated through, about 1 minute. Season with salt and pepper.

8. Drain the pasta, add it to the sauce, and toss everything together. Serve immediately, garnished with the Parmesan cheese.

TAGLIATELLE WITH RADICCHIO, WILD MUSHROOMS, LEEKS, AND PANCETTA

Serves 6

Pancetta is Italian bacon that is dry cured and has not been smoked. If it is not available, substitute prosciutto ham or bacon. If bacon is used, reduce the amount by half and omit the olive oil. Leeks are milder and slightly sweeter than onions. Small to medium leeks are the most tender; large leeks should be avoided. Leeks can harbor a considerable amount of dirt. Clean leeks by cutting them in half lengthwise and placing the halves under cold running water, separating the layers to wash away any grit.

1 recipe Basic Pasta Dough (page 143)
1½ cups Chicken Stock (page 138)
½ ounce dried porcini mushrooms
Flour for dusting
Cornmeal for dusting
1 tablespoon olive oil
¼ pound pancetta, finely diced
2 cloves garlic, minced
2 small leeks, white part only, thinly sliced

10 ounces fresh wild mushrooms, thinly sliced (chanterelle, shiitake, boletus, or oyster mushrooms)
1 small head radicchio, cored and sliced very thin
2 tablespoons chopped fresh parsley
2 tablespoons chopped fresh oregano
Salt and pepper
Toasted bread crumbs for garnish
Grated Parmesan cheese for garnish

1. Prepare the Basic Pasta Dough and set aside.
2. Bring the stock to a boil in a small saucepan. Add the porcini mushrooms; remove from the heat and let stand for 30 minutes.
3. Meanwhile, roll the pasta dough through a pasta machine, starting with the widest setting and working down to the next-to-last setting, dusting with flour when necessary to prevent sticking.
4. Cut the dough into 10- to 12-inch lengths and dust lightly with flour.
5. Run the dough through the tagliatelle cutter of the pasta machine, or cut the noodles by hand to a ¼-inch width. Place the pasta on a baking pan lined with a kitchen towel dusted with cornmeal, or hang on a pasta rack.
6. Strain the porcini mushrooms, setting aside the stock. Chop the porcini finely.
7. Heat the olive oil in a large sauté pan over medium heat. Add the pancetta and cook until crisp, about 10 minutes. Add the garlic and leeks; sauté for 3 to 4 minutes. Add the chopped porcini mushrooms and the sliced fresh mushrooms; cook until soft, 4 to 5 minutes, stirring occasionally. Add the radicchio, reserved stock, and herbs. Season with salt and pepper and cook for 1 minute. Set aside in a warm place.
8. Cook the pasta in salted boiling water for 1 to 2 minutes, until *al dente* or slightly firm to the bite.
9. Drain the pasta, add it to the mushroom mixture, and toss everything together. Divide among 6 serving plates and garnish with the bread crumbs and Parmesan cheese. Serve immediately.

TAGLIATELLE WITH LAMB, EGGPLANT, TOMATO, AND GREMOLATA

Serves 6

This rich and full-flavored dish is perfect as a first course on a winter menu. Gremolata is a mixture of parsley, garlic, and lemon zest used to garnish stews, soups, and pasta dishes. Sprinkled on top just before serving, it freshens the flavor of the dish. Make the gremolata as close to serving time as possible to provide the freshest flavor.

1 recipe Basic Pasta Dough (page 143)
4 tablespoons olive oil
¾ pound lamb leg or shoulder, trimmed of all fat and finely diced
2 cloves garlic, minced
1 bay leaf
4 tomatoes, peeled, seeded, and diced
4 cups Beef Stock (page 139) or lamb stock
Flour for dusting
Cornmeal for dusting

GREMOLATA
2 cloves garlic, minced
¼ cup chopped fresh parsley
Grated zest of 1 lemon

1 small eggplant, peeled and finely diced
2 tablespoons chopped fresh chives
1 tablespoon chopped fresh thyme
1 tablespoon chopped fresh oregano
Salt and pepper

1. Prepare the Basic Pasta Dough and set aside.
2. Heat 2 tablespoons of the olive oil in a large saucepan over medium-high heat. Add the lamb and cook until browned, stirring often. Add half the minced garlic (setting aside the remaining garlic for the gremolata), the bay leaf, tomato, and stock; bring to a boil, reduce the heat, and gently simmer until the meat is tender, about 1½ hours.
3. Meanwhile, roll the pasta dough through a pasta machine, starting with the widest setting and working down to the next-to-last setting, dusting with flour when necessary to prevent sticking.
4. Cut the dough into 10- to 12-inch lengths and dust lightly with flour.
5. Run the dough through the tagliatelle cutter of the pasta machine, or cut the noodles by hand to a ¼-inch width. Place the pasta on a baking pan lined with a kitchen towel dusted with cornmeal, or hang on a pasta rack.
6. *Prepare the gremolata:* Combine the garlic, the parsley, and lemon zest in a small bowl; set aside.
7. Heat the remaining 2 tablespoons olive oil in a sauté pan over medium-high heat. Add the eggplant and cook for 4 to 5 minutes, stirring often.
8. Add the eggplant mixture and herbs to the lamb mixture; cook for 2 to 3 minutes. Season with salt and pepper.
9. Cook the pasta in salted boiling water for 1 to 2 minutes, until *al dente* or slightly firm to the bite.
10. Drain the pasta, add it to the lamb-eggplant mixture, and toss everything together. Garnish with the gremolata and serve.

BREADS

ANADAMA BREAD

Makes 2 loaves

This slightly sweet bread has a lovely golden brown crust. When preparing the sponge, make sure to allow the hot cornmeal mixture to cool to lukewarm (100° to 110°) before stirring in the yeast. Too high a temperature may kill the yeast.

SPONGE	BREAD DOUGH
1 cup boiling water	1 cup milk, warmed
¾ cup cornmeal	1 tablespoon salt
1 cup Sourdough Starter (page 145)	1 cup whole wheat flour
1 tablespoon active dry yeast	4 to 5 cups unbleached bread flour
¼ cup molasses	1 egg beaten with 1 tablespoon water
1 cup unbleached bread flour	for egg wash

1. *Prepare the sponge:* Pour the boiling water into a large bowl. Slowly whisk in the cornmeal; let stand at room temperature until lukewarm. Stir in the starter, yeast, molasses, and flour; mix until smooth. Cover with a kitchen towel or plastic wrap and let stand at room temperature for 2 hours.

2. *Prepare the bread dough:* Using a wooden spoon, stir the milk, salt, whole wheat flour, and 2 cups of the bread flour into the sponge; mix until smooth. Continue to stir in small amounts of bread flour until the dough starts to come together and forms a ball.

3. Transfer the dough to a floured worktable and knead with your hands, adding more bread flour when necessary to prevent sticking. Knead until the dough is smooth and elastic, about 10 minutes. Transfer to an oiled bowl, cover, and let rise in a warm place (80° to 90°) until double in size, about 2 hours.

4. Punch down the dough and let rise for 30 minutes.

5. Divide the dough in half and shape into loaves. Line a baking pan with parchment paper. Place the loaves seam side down on the paper. (If baking on a stone, place the loaves on a wooden paddle dusted with cornmeal.) Allow to rise, covered, in a warm place until double in size, about 30 minutes.

6. Preheat the oven to 375°.

7. Cut a few slashes in the top of each loaf with a serrated knife. Brush with the egg wash and bake for 40 to 50 minutes. Tap the bottom of each loaf; it should produce a hollow sound when done. Let cool on a wire rack.

LEVAIN BREAD

Makes 3 loaves

This is the ultimate country peasant bread. It has a distinct mellow tang, a chewy texture, and an irregular, porous crumb. Levain bread refers to bread leavened without commercial yeast and prepared with a portion of the dough left from the previous baking. Use the leftover portion of dough instead of the starter for the next baking.

SPONGE
1 cup Sourdough Starter (page 145)
2 cups warm water
1 cup organic whole wheat flour
2 cups unbleached bread flour

BREAD DOUGH
2 cups warm water
1 tablespoon salt
7 to 8 cups unbleached bread flour

1. *Prepare the sponge:* Combine the starter, warm water, whole wheat flour, and bread flour in a large bowl. Stir together with a wooden spoon until thoroughly mixed. Cover with a kitchen towel or plastic wrap and let stand in a warm place (80° to 90°) for 3 hours. At this point you can remove 1 cup of the sponge for future baking. Store in a glass jar and refrigerate.
2. *Prepare the bread dough:* To the remaining sponge stir in the water, salt, and 3 cups of the bread flour; mix until smooth. Continue to add bread flour until the dough starts to come together and forms a ball.
3. Transfer the dough to a floured worktable and knead with your hands, adding more bread flour when necessary to prevent sticking. Knead until the dough is smooth and elastic, about 15 minutes. Transfer to an oiled bowl, cover with a kitchen towel, and allow to rise in a warm place until double in size, about 3 to 4 hours.
4. Grease three 9- by 5-inch loaf pans. Divide the dough into thirds, shape into loaves, and place in the prepared pans. Cover and let stand in a warm place until double in size, about 3 to 4 hours.
5. Preheat the oven to 400°.
6. Bake the loaves for 40 to 50 minutes. Tap the bottom of each loaf; it should produce a hollow sound when done. Let cool on a wire rack.

BLUE CHEESE, ONION, AND ROSEMARY BREAD

Makes 2 loaves

A fantastic aroma fills the kitchen when this bread is baking. The unusual combination of ingredients works well to produce a very flavorful bread with a wonderful richness and pronounced cheese flavor.

SPONGE
1 cup Sourdough Starter (page 145)
½ cup warm water
1 tablespoon active dry yeast
¾ cup unbleached bread flour

ONIONS
2 tablespoons unsalted butter
4 onions, peeled and diced
1 teaspoon sugar

BREAD DOUGH
1½ cups warm water
1 tablespoon salt
1 tablespoon olive oil
2 tablespoons honey
6 to 7 cups unbleached bread flour
¼ pound blue cheese, crumbled
4 tablespoons chopped fresh rosemary
1 egg beaten with 1 tablespoon water
  for egg wash

1. *Prepare the sponge:* Stir together the starter, warm water, yeast, and flour in a large bowl. Cover with a kitchen towel or plastic wrap and let stand at room temperature for 2 hours.
2. *Prepare the onions:* Warm the butter in a sauté pan over medium-high heat. Add the onions and sugar; cook until lightly browned, about 20 to 30 minutes, stirring often. Remove from heat and set aside.
3. *Prepare the bread dough:* Using a wooden spoon, stir the warm water, salt, olive oil, honey, and 1 cup of the bread flour into the sponge; mix until smooth. Continue to stir in flour until the dough starts to come together and forms a ball.
4. Transfer the dough to a floured worktable and knead, adding more bread flour when necessary to prevent sticking. Knead until the dough is smooth and elastic, about 10 minutes. Transfer to an oiled bowl, cover, and let rise in a warm place (80° to 90°) until double in size, about 2 hours.
5. Punch down the dough and let rise for another 30 minutes.
6. Divide the dough in half. With your fingertips press each piece into an 8- by 5-inch rectangle. Cover each rectangle with a layer of the onion mixture, then sprinkle with the cheese and rosemary. Roll up each loaf jelly-roll fashion.
7. Line a baking pan with parchment paper and place the loaves seam side down on the paper. (If using a baking stone, place the loaves on a wooden paddle dusted with cornmeal.) Cover the loaves and allow to rise in a warm place until double in size, about 20 to 30 minutes.
8. Preheat the oven to 375°.
9. Cut a few slashes in the top of each loaf with a serrated knife. Brush with the egg wash and bake for 40 to 50 minutes. Tap the bottom of each loaf; it should produce a hollow sound when done. Let cool on a wire rack.

ORANGE FENNEL WHOLE WHEAT BREAD

Makes 2 loaves

The orange zest and juice paired with the licorice flavor of the fennel make this otherwise straightforward whole wheat bread more interesting.

SPONGE
1 cup Sourdough Starter (page 145)
½ cup warm water
1 cup unbleached bread flour
1 tablespoon active dry yeast
Grated zest and juice of 2 oranges

BREAD DOUGH
1 cup warm water
1 tablespoon fennel seeds
1 tablespoon salt
2 tablespoons honey
2 cups whole wheat flour
3 to 4 cups unbleached bread flour
1 egg beaten with 1 tablespoon
    water for egg wash

1. *Prepare the sponge:* Stir together the starter, warm water, flour, yeast, and orange zest and juice in a large bowl. Cover with a kitchen towel or plastic wrap and let stand at room temperature for 2 hours.

2. *Prepare the bread dough:* Using a wooden spoon, stir the warm water, fennel, salt, honey, whole wheat flour, and 1 cup of the bread flour into the sponge; mix until smooth. Continue to stir in bread flour until the dough starts to come together and forms a ball.

3. Transfer the dough to a floured worktable and knead with your hands, adding more bread flour when necessary to prevent sticking. Knead until the dough is smooth and elastic, about 10 minutes. Transfer to an oiled bowl, cover, and let rise in a warm place (80° to 90°) until double in size, about 2 hours.

4. Punch down the dough and allow to rise for 30 minutes.

5. Divide the dough in half and shape into loaves. Line a baking pan with parchment paper and place the loaves on the paper. (If using a baking stone, place the loaves on a wooden paddle dusted with cornmeal.) Cover the loaves and allow to rise until double in size, about 20 minutes.

6. Preheat the oven to 375°.

7. Cut a few slashes in the top of each loaf using a serrated knife. Brush the loaves with egg wash and bake for 40 to 50 minutes. Tap the bottom of each loaf; it should produce a hollow sound when done. Let cool on a wire rack.

Boxed lunches in a bag

For the past 15 years, one of the best bargains on Deer Isle has been the Pilgrim's Inn box lunch. It has been so popular we haven't changed its basic contents. But we often tuck in other treasures from the Inn's refrigerator, such as slices of lamb, a ramekin of paté, or a wedge of almond torte. Many a picnic on the granite shores of Deer Isle has featured the little brown bags tied with a ribbon.

—Jean and Dud Hendrick

Menu for a Perfect Lunch

Celery and carrot sticks
Peanut butter on Ritz crackers
Trail mix (chocolate chips, raisins
    and unsalted peanuts)
Cheese, salami, and water crackers

Loaf of homemade bread
Pilgrim's Inn Chicken Salad
Fresh-baked cookies
Melon chunks

PILGRIM'S INN CHICKEN SALAD

Chop cooked chicken into small pieces. Add enough equal amounts of mayonnaise and sour cream to bind it together. Add a squeeze of orange juice and a dash of salt, pepper and curry. Finally, add enough finely chopped dates, figs, and crystallized ginger to make it interesting.

SOURDOUGH MILLET BREAD

Makes 2 loaves

Millet is a grain that gives bread a crunchy bite and a hint of sweetness. Toasting the millet will help bring out more of its delicate flavor. Toast it in a heavy skillet over medium-high heat until it is lightly browned.

SPONGE
1 cup Sourdough Starter (page 145)
1 cup milk, warmed
1 tablespoon active dry yeast
1 cup unbleached bread flour

BREAD DOUGH
1 cup warm water
2 tablespoons honey

1 tablespoon salt
½ cup millet, toasted
4 tablespoons butter, melted
1 cup whole wheat flour
3 to 4 cups unbleached bread flour
1 egg, beaten with 1 tablespoon
    water for egg wash

1. *Prepare the sponge:* Stir together the starter, milk, yeast, and flour in a large bowl. Cover with a kitchen towel or plastic wrap and let stand at room temperature for 2 hours.
2. *Prepare the bread dough:* Using a wooden spoon, stir the warm water, honey, salt, millet, butter, whole wheat flour, and 1 cup of the bread flour into the sponge; mix until smooth. Continue to stir in the bread flour until the dough starts to come together and forms a ball.
3. Transfer the dough to a floured worktable and knead with your hands, adding more bread flour when necessary to prevent sticking. Knead until the dough is smooth and elastic, about 10 minutes. Transfer to an oiled bowl, cover with a kitchen towel, and allow to rise in a warm place (80° to 90°) until double in size, about 2 hours.
4. Punch down the dough and let rise for another 30 minutes.
5. Divide the dough in half and shape into loaves. Line a baking pan with parchment paper. Place the loaves seam side down on the paper. (If baking on a stone, place the loaves on a wooden paddle dusted with cornmeal.) Allow the loaves to rise, covered, in a warm place until double in size, about 20 to 30 minutes.
6. Preheat the oven to 375°.
7. Cut a few slashes in the top of each loaf with a serrated knife. Brush the loaves with the egg wash and bake for 40 to 50 minutes. Tap the bottom of each loaf; it should produce a hollow sound when done. Let cool on a wire rack.

SOURDOUGH GARLIC AND
PARMESAN CHEESE BREAD

Makes 2 loaves

As this bread bakes, it fills the inn with the warm fragrance of garlic, Parmesan, and olive oil. The garlic flavor in this bread is mild, so for a more pronounced flavor, add an extra bulb. Chopped fresh herbs such as rosemary, basil, thyme, or savory would make a wonderful addition to this bread.

SPONGE
1 cup Sourdough Starter (page 145)
½ cup warm water
2 teaspoons active dry yeast
1 cup unbleached bread flour

BREAD DOUGH
2 bulbs garlic
8 tablespoons olive oil

¾ cup warm water
2 teaspoons salt
2 tablespoons honey
4 to 5 cups unbleached bread flour
½ cup grated Parmesan cheese
1 egg beaten with 1 tablespoon water for egg wash

1. *Prepare the sponge:* Stir together the starter, warm water, yeast, and flour in a large bowl. Cover with a kitchen towel or plastic wrap and let stand at room temperature for 2 hours.
2. *Prepare the bread dough:* Preheat the oven to 300°. Coat the garlic with 2 tablespoons of the olive oil and place in a small roasting pan. Cover with aluminum foil and bake for 1 hour. Remove from the oven and allow to cool for 30 minutes.
3. Cut a ½-inch slice off the top of each bulb using a serrated knife. Squeeze out the soft garlic and set aside.
4. Using a wooden spoon, stir the warm water, 4 tablespoons of the olive oil, the salt, honey, and 2 cups of the bread flour into the sponge; mix until smooth. Continue to stir in bread flour until the dough starts to come together and forms a ball.
5. Transfer the dough to a floured worktable and knead with your hands, adding more bread flour when necessary to prevent sticking. Knead until the dough is smooth and elastic, about 10 minutes. Transfer to an oiled bowl, cover, and allow to rise in a warm place (80° to 90°) until double in size, about 2 hours.
6. Punch down the dough and let rise for 30 minutes.
7. Divide the dough in half. With your fingertips press each piece into an 8- by 5-inch rectangle.
8. Whisk together the soft garlic and the remaining 2 tablespoons olive oil. Spread onto the dough rectangles. Top with the Parmesan cheese, then roll up jelly-roll fashion.
9. Line a baking pan with parchment paper. Place the loaves seam side down on the paper. (If using a baking stone, place the loaves on a wooden paddle dusted with cornmeal.) Cover the loaves and allow to rise in a warm place until double in size, about 20 to 30 minutes.

10. Preheat the oven to 375°.
11. Cut a few slashes in the top of each loaf with a serrated knife. Brush with the egg wash and bake for 40 to 50 minutes. Tap the bottom of each loaf; it should produce a hollow sound when done. Let cool on a wire rack.

ABOUT BREAD

Letting bread dough rise, or proof, allows time for the yeast cells to give off carbon dioxide gas, which expands and develops the dough. The rising time varies depending on the temperature and humidity of the day. To determine when the dough has risen sufficiently, you can press a finger into the dough; if the indentation remains, the dough is ready.

To store bread, make sure that it is thoroughly cooled, then place it in a paper bag and leave it at room temperature if it is to be eaten within 2 to 3 days. To keep bread longer than a few days, place it in the refrigerator. To freshen bread stored in the refrigerator, place it, unwrapped, in a 300° oven for 15 minutes.

Bread also freezes well and will keep for months if stored properly. To freeze bread, enclose it tightly in plastic wrap or aluminum foil, place it in a heavy plastic bag, and tie the bag securely. Defrost the bread at room temperature, then remove the wrappings, transfer it to a baking pan, and warm it in a 300° oven for 15 minutes.

SOURDOUGH PESTO AND SUN-DRIED TOMATO BREAD

Makes 2 loaves

This bread makes exceptional croutons for soups and salads. Slices of the bread can be rubbed with cut garlic, grilled, and served with pasta or used for crostini and bruschetta. If possible, make the pesto the same day as the bread.

SPONGE
¾ cup Sourdough Starter (page 145)
½ cup warm water
1 tablespoon active dry yeast
¾ cup unbleached bread flour

BREAD DOUGH
1 cup warm water
3 tablespoons olive oil

1 tablespoon salt
1 tablespoon honey
6 to 7 cups unbleached bread flour
2 tablespoons Pesto (page 143)
10 sun-dried tomatoes packed in oil, drained and finely diced
1 egg beaten with 1 teaspoon water for egg wash

1. *Prepare the sponge:* Stir together the starter, warm water, yeast, and flour in a large bowl. Cover with a kitchen towel or plastic wrap and let stand at room temperature for 2 hours.
2. *Prepare the bread dough:* Using a wooden spoon, stir the warm water, 1 tablespoon of the olive oil, the salt, honey, and 2 cups of the bread flour into the sponge; mix until smooth. Continue to stir in the bread flour until the dough starts to come together and forms a ball.
3. Transfer the dough to a floured worktable and knead with your hands, adding more bread flour when necessary to prevent sticking. Knead until the dough is smooth and elastic, about 10 minutes. Transfer to an oiled bowl, cover, and allow to rise in a warm place (80° to 90°) until double in size, about 2 hours.
4. Punch down the dough and allow to rise for 30 minutes.
5. Divide the dough in half. With your fingertips press each piece into a 10- by 5-inch rectangle.
6. Stir together the remaining 2 tablespoons olive oil and the pesto in a small bowl. Brush the rectangles with the pesto mixture and sprinkle with the sun-dried tomato. Roll up the rectangles jelly-roll fashion.
7. Line a baking pan with parchment paper. Place the loaves seam side down on the paper. (If using a baking stone, place the loaves on a wooden paddle dusted with cornmeal.) Cover the loaves and allow to rise in a warm place until double in size, about 30 minutes.
8. Preheat the oven to 375°.
9. Cut a few slashes in the top of each loaf with a serrated knife. Brush with the egg wash and bake for 40 to 50 minutes. Tap the bottom of each loaf; it should produce a hollow sound when done. Let cool on a wire rack.

BLACK OLIVE SOURDOUGH BREAD

Makes 2 loaves

SPONGE
1 cup Sourdough Starter (page 145)
½ cup warm water
1 tablespoon active dry yeast
1 cup unbleached bread flour

BREAD DOUGH
1 cup warm water
4 to 5 cups unbleached bread flour

3 tablespoons olive oil
4 teaspoons salt
¾ cup black olives, finely diced
2 tablespoons chopped fresh thyme
1 egg beaten with 1 tablespoon
   water for egg wash

1. *Prepare the sponge:* Stir together the starter, warm water, yeast, and flour in a large bowl. Cover with a kitchen towel or plastic wrap and let stand at room temperature for 2 hours.
2. *Prepare the bread dough:* Using a wooden spoon, stir the warm water, 1 cup of the bread flour, 1 tablespoon of the olive oil, and the salt into the sponge; mix until smooth. Continue to stir in bread flour until the dough starts to come together and forms a ball.
3. Transfer the dough to a floured worktable and knead with your hands, adding more bread flour when necessary to prevent sticking. Knead until the dough is smooth and elastic, about 10 minutes. Transfer to an oiled bowl, cover, and let rise in a warm place (80° to 90°) until double in size, about 2 hours.
4. Punch down the dough and let rise for another 30 minutes.
5. Divide the dough in half. With your fingertips press each piece into an 8- by 5-inch rectangle.
6. Brush the rectangles with the remaining 2 tablespoons olive oil. Sprinkle with the black olives and thyme, then roll up jelly-roll fashion.
7. Line a baking pan with parchment paper. Place the loaves seam side down on the paper. (If using a baking stone, place the loaves on a wooden paddle dusted with cornmeal.) Cover the loaves and allow to rise in a warm place until double in size, about 20 to 30 minutes.
8. Preheat the oven to 375°.
9. Cut a few slashes in the top of each loaf with a serrated knife. Brush with the egg wash and bake for 40 to 50 minutes. Tap the bottom of each loaf; it should produce a hollow sound when done. Let cool on a wire rack.

SOURDOUGH POTATO BREAD

Makes 3 loaves

Potato gives this bread a deliciously distinctive flavor and a moist, soft, and slightly chewy texture. The bread keeps well in the refrigerator or freezer and is excellent for toast and sandwiches.

SPONGE
1 cup Sourdough Starter (page 145)
½ cup warm water
1 tablespoon active dry yeast
1 cup unbleached bread flour

BREAD DOUGH
1 russet potato
¾ cup warm water

½ cup plain yogurt
2 tablespoons honey
1 tablespoon salt
7 to 8 cups unbleached bread flour
1 egg beaten with 1 tablespoon
    water for egg wash

1. *Prepare the sponge:* Stir together the starter, warm water, yeast, and flour in a large bowl. Cover with a kitchen towel or plastic wrap and let stand at room temperature for 2 hours.
2. *Prepare the bread dough:* Boil the potato until cooked through, about 15 to 20 minutes. When cool enough to handle, peel and mash the potato, then set aside to cool completely.
3. Using a wooden spoon, stir the warm water, yogurt, honey, salt, mashed potato, and 3 cups of the bread flour into the sponge; mix until smooth. Continue to stir in small amounts of bread flour until the dough starts to come together and forms a ball.
4. Transfer the dough to a floured worktable and knead with your hands, adding more bread flour when necessary to prevent sticking. Knead until the dough is smooth and elastic, about 10 minutes. Transfer to an oiled bowl, cover, and let rise in a warm place (80° to 90°) until double in size, about 2 hours.
5. Punch down the dough and let rise for 30 minutes.
6. Divide the dough into thirds and shape into loaves. Line a baking pan with parchment paper. Place the loaves seam side down on the paper. (If baking on a stone, place the loaves on a wooden paddle dusted with cornmeal.) Allow the loaves to rise, covered, in a warm place until double in size, 20 to 30 minutes.
7. Preheat the oven to 375°.
8. Cut a few slashes in the top of each loaf with a serrated knife. Brush with the egg wash and bake for 40 to 50 minutes. Tap the bottom of each loaf; it should produce a hollow sound when done. Let cool on a wire rack.

SEVEN-GRAIN SOURDOUGH BREAD

Makes 2 loaves

This flavorful, crusty bread is high in fiber. The seven-grain cereal gives the bread a coarse texture and grainy sweetness. Thinly sliced, it makes exceptionally good sandwiches and toast. Seven-grain cereal can be found in most natural food stores. The cereal contains soybeans, millet, wheat, buckwheat, triticale, corn, and oats.

SPONGE
1 cup Sourdough Starter (page 145)
½ cup warm water
1 tablespoon active dry yeast
½ cup unbleached bread flour
½ cup seven-grain cereal

BREAD DOUGH
1½ cups warm water
1 cup seven-grain cereal
4 teaspoons salt
3 tablespoons honey
4½ to 5½ cups unbleached bread flour
1 egg beaten with 1 tablespoon water
  for egg wash

1. *Prepare the sponge:* Stir together the starter, warm water, yeast, flour, and cereal in a large bowl. Cover with a kitchen towel or plastic wrap and let stand at room temperature for 2 hours.
2. *Prepare the bread dough:* Using a wooden spoon, stir the warm water, cereal, salt, honey, and 1 cup of the bread flour into the sponge; mix until smooth. Continue to stir in bread flour until the dough starts to come together and forms a ball.
3. Transfer the dough to a floured worktable and knead with your hands, adding more bread flour when necessary to prevent sticking. Knead until the dough is smooth and elastic, about 10 minutes. Transfer to an oiled bowl, cover, and let rise in a warm place (80° to 90°) until double in size, about 2 hours.
4. Punch down the dough and let rise for another 30 minutes.
5. Divide the dough in half and shape into loaves. Line a baking pan with parchment paper and place the loaves on the paper. (If using a baking stone, place the loaves on a wooden paddle dusted with cornmeal.) Cover the loaves and allow to rise in a warm place until double in size, about 20 minutes.
6. Preheat the oven to 375°.
7. Cut a few slashes in the top of each loaf using a serrated knife. Brush the loaves with the egg wash and bake for 40 to 50 minutes. Tap the bottom of each loaf; it should produce a hollow sound when done. Let cool on a wire rack.

SOURDOUGH RYE OATMEAL BREAD

Makes 2 loaves

This nutritious, satisfying bread has a creamy texture and rich, full flavor. It's ideal for toast and sandwiches. Rye flour gives this bread its dense, moist texture. Rye flour is almost always mixed with white flour because it does not contain enough gluten to entrap fermenting gas, which makes the bread rise. Always store rye and wheat flour in the refrigerator; allow them to come to room temperature before using. Oats give bread a slight sweetness and chewy crumb; pairing oats with whole wheat flour makes the bread taste richer.

SPONGE
1 cup boiling water
1 cup rolled oats
1 cup Sourdough Starter (page 145)
1 tablespoon active dry yeast
1 cup unbleached bread flour

BREAD DOUGH
1 cup buttermilk
1 cup rye flour
½ cup whole wheat flour
1 tablespoon salt
¼ cup honey
5 to 6 cups unbleached bread flour
1 egg beaten with 1 tablespoon water
  for egg wash

1. *Prepare the sponge:* Pour the boiling water over the oats in a large bowl and let cool until lukewarm. Stir in the starter, yeast, and flour; cover with a kitchen towel or plastic wrap and let stand at room temperature for 2 hours.

2. *Prepare the bread dough:* Using a wooden spoon, stir the buttermilk, rye and whole wheat flours, salt, and honey into the sponge; mix until smooth. Stir in the bread flour until the dough starts to come together and forms a ball.

3. Transfer the dough to a floured worktable and knead with your hands, adding more bread flour when necessary to prevent sticking. Knead until the dough is smooth and elastic, about 10 minutes. Transfer to an oiled bowl, cover, and let rise in a warm place (80° to 90°) until double in size, about 2 hours.

4. Punch down the dough and let rise for another 30 minutes.

5. Divide the dough in half and shape into round loaves. Line a baking pan with parchment paper and place the loaves on the paper. (If baking on a stone, place the loaves on a wooden paddle dusted with cornmeal.) Cover and let stand in a warm place until double in size, about 20 to 30 minutes.

6. Preheat the oven to 375°.

7. Cut a few slashes in the top of each loaf with a serrated knife. Brush with the egg wash and bake for 40 to 50 minutes. Tap the bottom of each loaf; it should produce a hollow sound when done. Let cool on a wire rack.

SALADS

POACHED CHICKEN, FENNEL, AND GRILLED ROMAINE SALAD

Serves 6

The crisp sweetness of the fennel and the tender, delicate flavor of the poached chicken contrast well with the smokiness of the grilled romaine. Poaching the chicken breast, grilling the romaine, and preparing the vinaigrette can all be done ahead of time. Toss everything with the vinaigrette as close to serving time as possible. Grilled radicchio would work well in this dish instead of, or in addition to, the romaine.

4 cups Court Bouillon (page 141)

VINAIGRETTE
¼ cup lemon juice (about 2 lemons)
1 clove garlic, minced
2 tablespoons chopped fresh dill
1 tablespoon chopped fresh parsley
1 teaspoon Dijon mustard
½ cup olive oil
Salt and pepper

SALAD
2 boneless, skinless chicken breasts
  (6 to 8 ounces each)
3 hearts of romaine lettuce
2 tablespoons olive oil
1 fennel bulb, trimmed, cored, and
  thinly sliced
10 ounces fresh mushrooms, cleaned
  and thinly sliced
¼ cup grated Parmesan cheese

1. Prepare the court bouillon and keep warm.
2. *Prepare the vinaigrette:* Combine the lemon juice, garlic, dill, parsley, and mustard in a small bowl. Slowly whisk in the olive oil. Season with salt and pepper and set aside.
3. Bring the court bouillon to a simmer; add the chicken breasts and poach until cooked all the way through, about 5 minutes. Remove the chicken and set aside to cool.
4. Cut the chicken into ¼-inch slices; place in a bowl and toss with a little of the vinaigrette. Set aside.
5. Prepare a charcoal grill.
6. Cut the romaine in half lengthwise, leaving the core intact. Brush both sides with the olive oil. Grill both sides until lightly browned, about 1 to 2 minutes per side. Remove from the grill and allow to cool.
7. Cut the romaine into ½-inch pieces; place in a bowl and toss with a little of the vinaigrette.
8. Combine the fennel and mushrooms in another bowl and toss with the remaining vinaigrette.
9. Divide the romaine among 6 serving plates. Place a portion of the fennel-mushroom mixture in the center of the romaine; arrange the chicken slices around the mixture. Sprinkle with the Parmesan cheese and serve.

LOBSTER AND SUMMER VEGETABLE SALAD IN RADICCHIO CUPS WITH CITRUS CHERVIL VINAIGRETTE

Serves 4

This colorful, refreshing salad is perfect to make in the summer when corn and beans are ready to harvest. The lobster, vegetables, and vinaigrette can be prepared ahead of time and tossed together just before serving.

1 lobster (1½ pounds)
1 cup haricots verts or other small green beans cut into 1-inch lengths, cooked
1 cup corn kernels, cooked (from 3 to 4 ears)
1 red bell pepper, thinly sliced
2 scallions, thinly sliced
6 to 8 whole radicchio leaves
½ head Bibb lettuce, thinly sliced
Chopped fresh chervil for garnish

VINAIGRETTE
2 lemons
2 limes
⅓ cup olive oil
3 tablespoons chopped fresh chervil
1 tablespoon chopped fresh parsley
1 shallot, finely diced
Salt and pepper

1. Steam or boil the lobster for 10 minutes. Remove from the heat and allow to cool.
2. Remove the lobster meat from the tail and claw sections. Dice the meat and place in a bowl. Add the beans, corn, bell pepper, and scallion; gently toss together.
3. *Prepare the vinaigrette:* Juice the lemons and limes into a small bowl and slowly whisk in the olive oil. Stir in the chervil, parsley, and shallot. Season with salt and pepper.
4. Pour the vinaigrette over the lobster-vegetable mixture and stir to coat.
5. Arrange the whole radicchio leaves in the center of each salad plate and top with the sliced Bibb lettuce. Top with the lobster mixture and serve garnished with chervil.

CAESAR SALAD WITH MARINATED GRILLED VEGETABLES

Serves 4 to 6

This versatile year-round salad can be served as a lunch entrée or as a first course for a fish or meat dinner. It is essential to use fresh vegetables; select those that are in peak season, and give consideration to color, flavor, and texture. The vegetables listed in this recipe should be used only as a guide. The choices are many: fennel, artichokes, leeks, mushrooms, yellow squash, potatoes, tomatoes, corn, and celeriac. The vinaigrette, croutons, and grilled vegetables can all be prepared in advance.

1 head romaine lettuce

VINAIGRETTE
2 cloves garlic, peeled
4 tablespoons lemon juice
1 teaspoon Dijon mustard
1 anchovy fillet
1 teaspoon capers
6 tablespoons olive oil
¼ cup grated Parmesan cheese
Salt and pepper

CROUTONS
3 tablespoons olive oil
2 cloves garlic, minced
1 cup French or Italian bread
   cubes (about ½-inch thick)
Salt and pepper

GRILLED VEGETABLES
1 small eggplant, cut into ¼-inch slices
1 small zucchini, cut in half lengthwise
½ pound asparagus, tough ends removed
1 bunch scallions, all but 2 inches of
   green part removed
1 red bell pepper, cut in half, seeded,
   stem removed
3 tablespoons olive oil
Salt and pepper
½ cup grated Parmesan cheese

1. Tear or cut the romaine into 2-inch pieces. Wash under cold water and dry in a salad spinner. Refrigerate until needed.
2. *Prepare the vinaigrette:* Place the garlic, lemon juice, mustard, anchovy, capers, and egg yolk in a food processor. Process for 30 seconds. With the motor running, slowly add the olive oil and process until smooth, about 1 minute. Add the Parmesan cheese and process for 30 seconds. Season with salt and pepper. Transfer to a bowl and refrigerate until needed.
3. Preheat the oven to 400°.
4. *Prepare the croutons:* Warm the olive oil in a small saucepan over medium heat. Add the garlic and cook just until it starts to brown. Remove from heat and allow to stand for 10 minutes.
5. Strain the garlic oil into a bowl; discard the garlic. Add the bread cubes to the garlic oil and toss to coat. Season with salt and pepper. Transfer the bread cubes

to a baking pan and bake until lightly brown, about 15 minutes, stirring occasionally. Remove from the oven and transfer to paper towels.

6. Prepare a charcoal grill.

7. *Prepare the grilled vegetables:* Brush the eggplant, zucchini, asparagus, scallions, and bell pepper with the olive oil. Season with salt and pepper and grill over a medium-high fire. Remove the vegetables and allow to cool slightly.

8. Toss the grilled vegetables with a little of the vinaigrette and let marinate for 30 minutes.

9. Place the chilled romaine in a large bowl and add half of the Parmesan. Add the vinaigrette and reserved croutons; toss until the lettuce is well coated.

10. Place a portion of the romaine on each salad plate and arrange the grilled vegetables around it. Garnish with the remaining Parmesan cheese and serve.

ABOUT SALADS

After washing salad greens, it is essential to thoroughly dry them. Water left on lettuce will not only wilt the leaves but dilute and change the flavor of the dressing. We have found that the best way to dry lettuce is with a salad spinner. Also, when dressing a salad always dress on the light side and immediately before serving.

PILGRIM'S INN GARDEN SALAD

Serves 4 to 6

We take great pride in our garden salad. The comments of our guests indicate that it is altogether different from what most expect of a house salad. Watching Jean gathering lettuces, herbs, and flowers from the garden is like watching a meticulous artist at work. She carefully combines a variety of flavors, shapes, colors, and textures, balancing mild leaf lettuces with bitter chicories, spicy arugula with delicate butterhead lettuce, and bright flowers with subtle herbs.

VINAIGRETTE
1 tablespoon white wine vinegar
2 tablespoons lemon juice
2 teaspoons chopped fresh chervil
2 teaspoons chopped fresh chives
2 teaspoons chopped fresh parsley
6 tablespoons olive oil
Salt and pepper

6 to 8 cups assorted garden lettuces, herbs, and flowers (oakleaf, romaine, butterhead, mâche, cress, arugula, sorrel, chicory, radicchio, mizuna, mint, basil, nasturtiums, calendula)

1. *Prepare the vinaigrette:* Combine the vinegar, lemon juice, and herbs in a bowl. Slowly whisk in the olive oil and season with salt and pepper.
2. Wash and thoroughly spin-dry the lettuces, herbs, and flowers. Place in a salad bowl and lightly toss with the vinaigrette, adding just enough to coat the greens. Serve immediately.

POACHED SEA SCALLOP SALAD WITH WATERCRESS AND CUCUMBER

Serves 2 to 4

The peppery watercress works well with the richness of the scallops and the cool, refreshing cucumbers to give this salad a wonderful combination of flavors. If the cucumbers have not been waxed, it is not necessary to peel them. If left unpeeled, wash them thoroughly in cold water. Refrigerating the cucumbers after slicing them will keep them crisp; remove them from the refrigerator just before serving. The scallops can be poached and the vinaigrette prepared well ahead of time.

4 cups Court Bouillon (page 141)
½ pound sea scallops, side muscle
  removed

VINAIGRETTE
2 tablespoons lemon juice
½ teaspoon Dijon mustard
1 tablespoon chopped fresh tarragon
1 clove garlic, minced
1 shallot, minced
4 tablespoons olive oil
Salt and pepper

SALAD
1 bunch watercress, thick stems
  removed
½ cucumber, peeled and thinly sliced
½ red onion, peeled and thinly sliced
½ red bell pepper, seeded and thinly
  sliced

1. Prepare the court bouillon. Add the scallops and poach for 3 to 5 minutes depending on the size of the scallops. Transfer the scallops to a bowl and set aside to cool.
2. *Prepare the vinaigrette:* In a small bowl stir together the lemon juice, mustard, tarragon, garlic, and shallot. Slowly whisk in the olive oil. Season with salt and pepper; set aside.
3. *Prepare the salad:* Combine the watercress, cucumber, onion, and bell pepper. Pour in half of the vinaigrette and toss until the vegetables are evenly coated.
4. Toss the remaining vinaigrette with the scallops.
5. Place a portion of the vegetable mixture on each serving plate and top with the scallops. Serve immediately.

Salad from Jean

For as long as I can remember, I have loved gardening. No matter where I went—from city lots to large plots—I managed to find a spot to grow something. Jody Bond, my former restaurant partner in Annapolis, taught me the value of using fresh herbs and flowers in cooking. In Maine, Stanley Joseph, an excellent gardener, introduced me and the Inn to dazzling and unusual new greens. A small garden was all I could manage when I was the Inn's chef, but since Terry's arrival, my gardens and greenhouse have flourished and can now supply our kitchen every day with greens, herbs, and garnishes. Maine's weather is ideal for growing the mesclun mix for our salads—a signature course of the Inn's dinners. A night doesn't go by without calendula and Rugosa rose petals gracing the plates, and a butter dish doesn't leave the kitchen without the accent of a Johnny-jump-up. My garden's bounty has become an essential part of the Inn's kitchen. The personal reward is pure joy.

—*Jean Hendrick*

SPINACH SALAD WITH MAINE CRAB AND AVOCADO

Serves 5

This delicate, exquisite salad is visually appealing as well as pleasing to the palate. It is an excellent salad for summer when crab is in season and avocados are ripe. It can be served as an appetizer or as a light lunch entrée. The avocado and crab can be prepared and placed in the ramekins a few hours ahead of time, then covered and refrigerated until needed.

AVOCADO MIXTURE
1 avocado
1 jalapeño pepper, minced
2 tablespoons chopped fresh cilantro
1 tablespoon chopped fresh parsley
Juice of ½ lime
1 teaspoon olive oil
Salt and pepper

CRAB MIXTURE
1 tablespoon mayonnaise,
  preferably homemade
Juice of 1 lime
1 clove garlic, minced
Salt and pepper
6 ounces crabmeat

VINAIGRETTE
2 tablespoons lemon juice
1 tablespoon lime juice
1 tablespoon chopped fresh cilantro
1 tablespoon chopped fresh parsley
3 tablespoons olive oil
Salt and pepper

SALAD
8 ounces spinach, washed, stems
  removed, leaves thinly sliced
1 red bell pepper, thinly sliced
3 scallions, thinly sliced

1. *Prepare the avocado mixture:* Peel the avocado, remove and discard the pit, and mash the flesh in a bowl until it has a fairly smooth consistency. Stir in the jalapeño, cilantro, parsley, lime juice, and olive oil. Season with salt and pepper and set aside.
2. *Prepare the crab mixture:* Stir together the mayonnaise, lime juice, and garlic in a bowl. Season with salt and pepper. Fold in the crabmeat and set aside.
3. *Prepare the vinaigrette:* Combine the lemon juice, lime juice, and herbs in a bowl. Slowly whisk in the olive oil and season with salt and pepper. Set aside.
4. Line five 2- or 3-ounce ramekins with plastic wrap. Evenly divide the avocado mixture among the five ramekins. Divide the crab mixture into five portions and place on top of the avocado. Press down on the crab with a spatula to slightly compress the mixture.
5. *Prepare the salad:* Combine the spinach, bell pepper, and scallion in a bowl. Toss with the vinaigrette. Divide the spinach mixture among 5 salad plates. Invert the crab-avocado mixture in the center of each plate. Serve immediately.

WARM GOAT CHEESE AND ROASTED RED BELL PEPPER SALAD WITH PAN-FRIED EGGPLANT

Serves 4

This salad could well serve as an appetizer to a grilled chicken entrée. The warm, creamy goat cheese, crisp eggplant, and sweet roasted peppers create a wonderful mix of textures and flavors. Roasting the pepper and breading the goat cheese and eggplant can be done ahead of time. The eggplant may be grilled, broiled, or sautéed instead of fried.

1 red bell pepper	Salt and pepper
1 log (4 ounces) goat cheese	1½ cups all-purpose flour
¾ cup olive oil	2 eggs, beaten with 2 tablespoons water
2 cups bread crumbs, preferably homemade	1 small eggplant, cut into ¼-inch-thick rounds, rounds cut in half
3 tablespoons balsamic vinegar	4 large handfuls mixed greens, such as romaine, arugula, cress, and spinach
1 shallot, minced	4 scallions, thinly sliced
1 teaspoon Dijon mustard	¼ cup grated Parmesan cheese
1 tablespoon chopped fresh thyme	

1. Place the bell pepper over a charcoal fire, under the broiler, or over a gas flame. Roast until the skin is uniformly charred, turning the pepper as needed. Place the pepper in a plastic bag, seal tightly, and allow to steam for 30 minutes. Remove the pepper from the bag, peel away the skin, cut the pepper in half, and discard the seeds and stem. Cut the pepper into thin strips and set aside.

2. Preheat the oven to 400°.

3. Cut the goat cheese into four ¾-inch rounds. Brush the rounds with 3 table-spoons of the olive oil, then lightly coat with ½ cup of the bread crumbs. Place the coated rounds on a baking pan and bake until lightly browned, about 6 to 8 minutes. Keep warm.

4. *Prepare the vinaigrette:* Stir together the vinegar, shallot, mustard, and thyme in a small bowl. Slowly whisk in 5 tablespoons of the olive oil. Season with salt and pepper and set aside.

5. Meanwhile, place the remaining 1½ cups bread crumbs, flour, and egg mixture in 3 separate bowls. Season the flour and bread crumbs with salt and pepper. Bread the eggplant by first coating with flour, then dipping in the egg mixture, then coating with the bread crumbs.

6. Heat the remaining 4 tablespoons olive oil in a skillet over medium-high heat until very hot. Add the breaded eggplant and cook until well browned on both sides. Transfer to a plate lined with paper towels.

7. Combine the mixed greens and scallions in a salad bowl and toss with half of the vinaigrette. Divide among 4 salad plates.

8. Place the warm goat cheese in the center of each plate. Arrange the eggplant slices and bell pepper strips around the cheese. Drizzle the remaining vinaigrette over the salad. Garnish with the Parmesan cheese and serve.

MUSSEL, CORN, AND ROASTED RED POTATO SALAD WITH ARUGULA

Serves 4 to 6

Here is a refreshing, colorful salad that makes a good first course for a summer dinner. Substitute lobster or scallops for the mussels, or add artichokes, fresh mushrooms, or leeks. Use your imagination and choose what is fresh and in season. The success of this salad depends on the quality of the corn; it must be as fresh as possible. The mussels, vegetables, and vinaigrette can be prepared in advance and tossed together just before serving.

6 red potatoes
2 cloves garlic, peeled and left whole,
    plus 2 cloves garlic, minced
2 tablespoons olive oil
2 sprigs fresh rosemary
Salt and pepper
1 pound mussels, debearded and
    scrubbed
¼ cup dry white wine
1 cup corn kernels, cooked
    (from 3 to 4 ears)
4 scallions, finely sliced
2 tablespoons capers

4 tablespoons chopped fresh tarragon
2 tablespoons chopped fresh parsley
2 tablespoons chopped fresh chives
2 bunches arugula (4 ounces each),
    washed and dried

VINAIGRETTE
3 tablespoons lemon juice
1 tablespoon raspberry vinegar
½ teaspoon Dijon mustard
5 tablespoons olive oil
Salt and pepper

1. Preheat the oven to 375°.
2. Combine the potatoes, whole garlic, olive oil, and rosemary in a roasting pan. Season with salt and pepper; roast until the potatoes are cooked through, about 30 to 40 minutes, stirring occasionally. Remove from the oven and allow to cool.
3. Meanwhile, place the mussels, wine, and minced garlic in a large saucepan. Cover and cook over medium-high heat until the mussels open, about 8 to 10 minutes, shaking the pan occasionally.
4. Remove the pan from the heat and allow to cool. Remove the mussels from the shells and place in a large bowl. Discard the shells.
5. When the potatoes have cooled, cut them into quarters and add them to the mussels. Add the corn, scallions, capers, and herbs; toss together.
6. *Prepare the vinaigrette:* Whisk together the lemon juice, vinegar, and mustard in a small bowl. Slowly whisk in the olive oil until smooth. Season with salt and pepper.
7. Toss the mussel mixture with all but 2 tablespoons of the vinaigrette.
8. Arrange a layer of arugula on each salad plate. Place a portion of the mussel mixture in the center of the arugula. Drizzle the reserved 2 tablespoons vinaigrette over the arugula and serve.

SESAME SNOW PEA SALAD WITH MIZUNA

Both light and easy to prepare, this salad has a touch of Asian flavor with tender and crisp textures. Mizuna is a mild-flavored Japanese mustard. If mizuna is not available, substitute any delicate salad green such as mâche or oakleaf lettuce. Other vegetables that would work well in this dish include broccoli, asparagus, cauliflower, or zucchini.

VINAIGRETTE
3 tablespoons rice wine vinegar
  or champagne vinegar
1 tablespoon soy sauce
Few drops sesame oil
2 teaspoons chopped fresh ginger
1 jalapeño pepper, minced
1 clove garlic, minced
2 shallots, minced
1 teaspoon Chinese or Dijon
  mustard
5 tablespoons peanut oil
Ground black pepper
6 ounces snow peas, ends trimmed
  and strings removed

1 red bell pepper, sliced into ¼-inch-wide
  strips
4 scallions, thinly sliced
2 carrots, thinly sliced
4 ounces white mushrooms, thinly sliced
1 stalk celery, thinly sliced
2 tablespoons chopped fresh parsley
4 tablespoons chopped fresh cilantro
2 tablespoons chopped fresh chives
1 bunch mizuna (about 4 handfuls),
  washed and dried
2 tablespoons sesame seeds, toasted

1. *Prepare the vinaigrette:* Whisk together the vinegar, soy sauce, sesame oil, ginger, jalapeño, garlic, shallots, and mustard in a bowl. Slowly whisk in the peanut oil and season with black pepper. Set aside.
2. Blanch the snow peas in boiling water for 30 seconds. Drain and place them in ice water to stop the cooking process; drain and let dry on paper towels. Transfer to a large bowl.
3. Add the bell pepper, scallions, carrots, mushrooms, celery, parsley, cilantro, and chives. Pour about three-quarters of the vinaigrette over the vegetable mixture and toss to coat.
4. Place a layer of mizuna on each salad plate. Arrange a portion of the marinated vegetables in the center of each plate. Drizzle the remaining vinaigrette over the mizuna. Garnish with the toasted sesame seeds and serve.

CITRUS BASIL VINAIGRETTE

Makes about 1 cup

Citrus and basil make an excellent vinaigrette for salads and also complement fish and chicken.

½ cup tightly packed fresh
   basil leaves, chopped
1 tablespoon chopped fresh parsley
2 tablespoons lime juice
2 tablespoons lemon juice

1 shallot, chopped
1 clove garlic, minced
½ cup olive oil
Salt and pepper

Purée the basil, parsley, lime and lemon juice, shallot, and garlic in a blender. With the motor running, slowly pour in the olive oil and mix until well blended. Season with salt and pepper.

CHAMPAGNE DILL VINAIGRETTE

Makes about 1 cup

When a mild vinegar such as champagne vinegar is used in a vinaigrette, it should be paired with tender, delicate salad greens.

1 tablespoon chopped fresh dill
1 tablespoon chopped fresh chives
¼ cup Champagne vinegar
1 shallot, minced

½ cup safflower oil
1 tablespoon olive oil
Salt and pepper

Combine the dill, chives, vinegar, and shallot in a small bowl. Slowly whisk in the oils until well blended. Season with salt and pepper.

MINT LIME VINAIGRETTE WITH WALNUT OIL

Makes about 1 cup

At Pilgrim's Inn we use this tasty combination to dress a salad of spinach, walnuts, and Roquefort cheese.

2 tablespoons chopped fresh mint
1 tablespoon chopped fresh chervil
1 tablespoon chopped fresh parsley
2 tablespoons lime juice (about 2 limes)
1 teaspoon grated lime zest

2 tablespoons champagne vinegar
1 scallion, finely diced
1 tablespoon walnut oil
½ cup safflower oil
Salt and pepper

Combine the mint, chervil, parsley, lime juice, lime zest, vinegar, and scallion in a small bowl. Slowly whisk in the oils until thoroughly blended. Season with salt and pepper.

CREAMY RASPBERRY DIJON VINAIGRETTE

Makes about 1 cup

This sharp and sweet vinaigrette stands up to sturdy-leaved greens, such as radicchio, escarole, frisée, and endive.

1 tablespoon chopped fresh tarragon
1 tablespoon chopped fresh parsley
1 tablespoon chopped fresh chives
¼ cup raspberry vinegar
1 shallot, finely diced

1 clove garlic, finely diced
1 tablespoon Dijon mustard
½ cup olive oil
Salt and pepper

Place the tarragon, parsley, chives, vinegar, shallot, garlic, and mustard in a blender or food processor and purée until smooth. With the motor running, slowly pour in the olive oil and mix until well blended. Season with salt and pepper.

NASTURTIUM VINAIGRETTE

Makes 1½ cups

Try this subtle vinaigrette on young and tender lettuces tossed with nasturtium leaves and mild-tasting herbs such as burnet, chervil, and lemon thyme.

½ cup good-quality white wine vinegar
½ cup nasturtium flowers
1 tablespoon chopped fresh chervil

1 cup safflower oil
Salt and pepper

1. In a small saucepan over medium-high heat, warm the vinegar to about 180°.
2. Place the nasturtium flowers in a bowl and pour in the warm vinegar. Cover and allow to steep for 24 hours.
3. Strain the vinegar into another bowl and discard the flowers. Stir in the chervil. Slowly whisk in the oil and season with salt and pepper.

MAIN COURSES

LOBSTER CRAB CAKES WITH WASABI RÉMOULADE SAUCE

Serves 4

These are essentially Maryland crab cakes made with Maine lobster and crab. Maine crabmeat comes from rock crabs, which have a sweeter and more delicate flavor than Maryland crabmeat, which comes from blue crabs. Depending on the moisture content of the crab and lobster, it may be necessary to add more bread crumbs to the mixture so that it can be formed into cakes. To make crab cakes without the lobster, follow this recipe and replace the lobster with ½ pound of crabmeat. Wasabi powder is Japanese horseradish and can be found in the Asian foods section of most well-stocked supermarkets.

CRAB CAKES
1 lobster (1½ pounds)
4 tablespoons olive oil
2 shallots, finely diced
½ stalk celery, finely diced
1 jalapeño pepper, finely diced
½ cup mayonnaise,
  preferably homemade
1 egg plus 2 egg whites
2 tablespoons chopped fresh parsley
2 tablespoons chopped fresh chervil
2 tablespoons chopped fresh chives
2 teaspoons Worcestershire sauce
1 teaspoon Old Bay seafood seasoning
1 teaspoon Dijon mustard
1 tablespoon capers
2 tablespoons bread crumbs
1 pound crabmeat
Salt and pepper

RÉMOULADE SAUCE
1 cup mayonnaise, preferably
  homemade
2 teaspoons wasabi powder
4 cornichons, minced
1 clove garlic, minced
1 scallion, minced
1 tablespoon capers
Juice of ½ lemon
1 tablespoon Dijon mustard
1 tablespoon Worcestershire sauce
Pinch of cayenne pepper
1 tablespoon chopped fresh parsley
1 tablespoon chopped fresh chervil
1 tablespoon chopped fresh tarragon
1 tablespoon chopped fresh chives
Salt and pepper

1. Steam or boil the lobster for 10 minutes. Remove from heat and let stand until cool enough to handle. Crack the claws, knuckles, and tail section and remove the meat. Finely dice the meat and set aside.
2. Heat 1 tablespoon of the olive oil in a small sauté pan. Add the shallots, celery, and jalapeño pepper. Sauté until the vegetables are soft, about 2 to 3 minutes. Set aside to cool.
3. Preheat the oven to 350°.
4. Whisk together the mayonnaise and whole egg in a large mixing bowl. Stir in the fresh herbs, Worcestershire, seafood seasoning, mustard, capers, sautéed vegetables, bread crumbs, crabmeat, and the reserved lobster meat. Season with salt and pepper.

5. In another bowl beat the egg whites to soft peaks. Gently fold into the lobster mixture.
6. Divide the mixture into 8 portions. Form into cakes 3 inches in diameter.
7. Heat the remaining 3 tablespoons olive oil in a large nonstick sauté pan over medium-high heat. Fry the cakes on both sides until lightly browned, about 1 minute per side.
8. Transfer the cakes to a baking pan and bake for 10 minutes.
9. *Meanwhile, prepare the rémoulade sauce:* Combine all the sauce ingredients in a small bowl and stir together until thoroughly blended.
10. Place 2 cakes on each serving plate. Serve with the sauce on the side.

ROASTED SALMON WITH SESAME GINGER CRUST AND SWEET AND SOUR LEEKS

Serves 4

The salmon can be prepared in advance, then covered and refrigerated until needed. At Pilgrim's Inn we use aquacultured salmon, which has a refined and delicate flavor. One of the most versatile fish available, it can be prepared in a variety of ways: poached, grilled, sautéed, roasted, or steamed. Tuna and swordfish can be used successfully in this dish if salmon is not available.

2 tablespoons finely diced fresh ginger
2 tablespoons sesame seeds, toasted
4 salmon fillets (about 6 ounces each)
4 tablespoons butter, melted
Ground black pepper

3 leeks, white part only, thinly sliced
2 teaspoons brown sugar
2 teaspoons Champagne vinegar
2 tablespoons water

1. Preheat the oven to 350°.
2. In a small bowl combine the ginger and sesame seeds.
3. Brush the salmon fillets with 2 tablespoons of the butter. Spread an even layer of the ginger mixture on the top of each fillet. Season with black pepper.
4. Place the fillets, seasoned side up, in a greased baking pan; bake until the fish is firm to the touch and moist on the inside, about 10 to 12 minutes.
5. Meanwhile, heat the remaining 2 tablespoons butter in a sauté pan over medium heat. Add the leek and cook for 2 to 3 minutes, stirring occasionally. Add the brown sugar, vinegar, and water; continue to cook until most of the liquid has evaporated, about 3 to 4 minutes.
6. Place a portion of the leek mixture in the center of each serving plate and top with a salmon fillet. Serve immediately.

ROASTED SALMON IN PHYLLO
WITH CELERIAC PURÉE

Well suited for a large group of people, this tasty, savory pastry is simple to prepare and can be put together ahead of time. The phyllo dough keeps the salmon moist and hot after it is taken out of the oven. Keeping the dough covered with a damp towel while working with it prevents it from drying out and becoming brittle. Phyllo dough can be found in the frozen-food section of most supermarkets.

1 pound celeriac, peeled and chopped
Salt and pepper
3 tablespoons heavy cream or milk
2 tablespoons unsalted butter plus
   melted butter for brushing phyllo

12 sheets phyllo
6 salmon fillets (about 5 ounces
   each)

1. Place the celeriac in a saucepan, cover with water, add a pinch of salt, and cook until soft, about 10 to 12 minutes.
2. Drain the water from the pan. Run the celeriac through a food mill or mash it with a fork. Return the celeriac to the pan and stir in the cream and the 2 tablespoons butter. Cook over medium heat for 2 minutes. Season with salt and pepper and set aside to cool.
3. Lay 1 sheet of phyllo on a worktable and lightly brush with the melted butter. Top with another sheet of phyllo and brush with butter. Fold the sheets in half and brush the top with butter.
4. Place 1 salmon fillet along the lower lengthwise third of the phyllo. Spread 2 tablespoons of the celeriac mixture on top of the salmon. Fold in the left and right sides of the phyllo to slightly cover the ends of the salmon.
5. Roll up the phyllo jelly-roll fashion and place it seam side down on an ungreased baking pan. Brush the top with butter. Repeat with the remaining salmon and phyllo. Refrigerate the salmon rolls for 1 hour.
6. Preheat the oven to 400°. Bake the salmon so that it is slightly firm and still moist on the inside, about 20 to 25 minutes.
7. Cut each salmon roll in half with a serrated knife and serve.

SAUTÉED SALMON CAKES WITH RED WINE BALSAMIC VINEGAR BUTTER SAUCE

Serves 4

This is an ideal way to use any leftover pieces of salmon from filleting a whole fish. It is essential to slightly undercook the salmon when poaching it; this prevents the salmon cakes from drying out and also enhances the salmon flavor. The cakes can be prepared in advance, then covered and refrigerated until needed. The sauce must be made as close to serving time as possible and kept in a warm place (110°) until needed. If the sauce becomes too hot or too cold, it will separate.

1 carrot, finely diced
1 stalk celery, finely diced
1 small onion, finely diced
1 tablespoon chopped fresh parsley
1 cup dry white wine
6 cups water
1 teaspoon salt
1 teaspoon black peppercorns
1 teaspoon lemon juice
1 pound salmon fillet
1 russet potato
3 tablespoons olive oil
3 shallots, finely diced
1 clove garlic, minced

1 teaspoon chopped fresh ginger
½ teaspoon curry powder
2 eggs, beaten
2 tablespoons chopped fresh dill
2 tablespoons chopped fresh chives
Salt and pepper

RED WINE BALSAMIC SAUCE
½ cup good-quality dry red wine
¼ cup balsamic vinegar
1 shallot, finely minced
6 tablespoons unsalted butter, softened
Salt and pepper
1 teaspoon chopped fresh dill

1. Place the carrot, celery, onion, parsley, wine, water, salt, peppercorns, and lemon juice in a large saucepan. Bring to a boil; reduce the heat and simmer for 15 minutes. Add the salmon and poach for 4 to 5 minutes; it should be slightly undercooked. Remove the salmon and set aside to cool.

2. Place the potato in a small saucepan and cover with water; bring to a boil and cook until soft, about 15 minutes. Remove the potato and allow to cool slightly.

3. Heat 1 tablespoon of the olive oil in a sauté pan over medium heat. Add the shallots, garlic, ginger, and curry powder; sauté for 2 minutes, stirring occasionally. Remove from heat and allow to cool.

4. Peel the potato while it is slightly warm and put it through a food mill, or mash with a fork. Transfer to a large bowl and stir in the sautéed shallot mixture. Flake the salmon and stir it into the mixture. Stir in the eggs, dill, and chives; mix well. Season with salt and pepper.

5. Divide the mixture into 8 equal portions and form into cakes 3 inches in diameter. Refrigerate the cakes for 1 hour.

6. Preheat the oven to 350°.

7. Heat the remaining 2 tablespoons olive oil in a large sauté pan over medium-high heat. Sauté the cakes on both sides until they are lightly browned. Transfer to a greased baking pan and bake for 10 minutes.

8. *Meanwhile, prepare the sauce:* Combine the wine, balsamic vinegar, and shallot in a small saucepan; cook over medium-high heat until the mixture is reduced to 2 tablespoons. Turn the heat to low and slowly whisk in the butter a few pieces at a time. Do not allow the sauce to boil. Season with salt and pepper and the dill.

9. Divide the sauce onto serving plates and top with 2 salmon cakes per plate. Serve immediately.

GRILLED HALIBUT WITH LEMON BASIL VINAIGRETTE

Serves 6

We have found that halibut from the East Coast, specifically from Maine, is far superior to western halibut. This cold-water species has a faintly sweet, delicate flavor. Other firm white-fleshed fish such as grouper, turbot, cod, or haddock would also work well in this dish.

VINAIGRETTE
1 teaspoon Dijon mustard
3 tablespoons lemon juice (1 to 2 lemons)
3 tablespoons chopped fresh basil
1 tablespoon chopped fresh parsley
1 tablespoon capers
1 clove garlic, minced
½ cup olive oil
1 tomato, peeled, seeded, and chopped
Salt and pepper

6 halibut fillets (about 6 ounces each)
¼ cup olive oil
Salt and pepper

Fresh basil leaves for garnish

1. Prepare a charcoal grill.
2. *Prepare the vinaigrette:* Place the mustard, lemon juice, basil, parsley, capers, and garlic in a food processor and process for 30 seconds. With the motor running, slowly pour in the olive oil; process for 1 minute. Scrape the mixture into a bowl and stir in the tomato. Season with salt and pepper and set aside.
3. Lightly coat the fillets with the olive oil; season with salt and pepper. Grill the fillets until firm, about 3 to 4 minutes per side.
4. Place the fillets on serving plates and spoon a little vinaigrette over each. Serve garnished with basil.

SAUTÉED SEA SCALLOPS WITH PORTABELLO MUSHROOMS, SPINACH, AND CABERNET SAUVIGNON

Serves 3

Because scallops are quite edible when raw, it is much better to undercook rather than overcook them. They should not be cooked ahead of time, for this greatly diminishes the tenderness and flavor. This is a complex and time-consuming preparation, so it is better suited to an intimate dinner.

Juice of 1 lemon
6 tablespoons olive oil
Salt and pepper
1 pound sea scallops, side muscle removed
12 ounces spinach, washed and stemmed
1 clove garlic, minced
2 shallots, finely diced

3 ounces fresh portabello mushrooms, finely diced
½ cup Cabernet Sauvignon or other good-quality dry red wine
1 teaspoon chopped fresh thyme
1 tablespoon chopped fresh parsley
2 tablespoons chopped fresh chives
¼ pound unsalted butter, softened
1 teaspoon balsamic vinegar

1. Whisk together the lemon juice and 4 tablespoons of the olive oil in a large bowl. Season with salt and pepper. Add the scallops and stir to coat. Refrigerate for 4 hours.
2. Steam the spinach until wilted, about 2 to 3 minutes. Allow to cool, then squeeze out as much liquid as possible; chop and set aside.
3. Heat 1 tablespoon of the olive oil in a large sauté pan. Add the garlic and shallots; sauté for 1 to 2 minutes. Add the chilled scallops and the mushrooms; cook for 4 to 5 minutes, stirring occasionally.
4. Remove the scallops and vegetables from the pan; keep warm in a low oven.
5. Add the wine to the pan and cook over medium-high heat until it is reduced to 2 tablespoons. Turn the heat to low; stir in the herbs, and slowly whisk in the butter a few pieces at a time. Season with salt and pepper and set aside in a warm place.
6. In another sauté pan heat the remaining 1 tablespoon olive oil over medium-high heat. Add the chopped spinach and cook until heated through. Season with salt and pepper and the vinegar.
7. Divide the spinach mixture among the serving plates. Top with the scallops and vegetables. Spoon a little of the wine sauce over the scallops and serve.

Scallops from Pearl Hardie

Though Pearl Hardie is uncertain exactly when his ancestors first came to Penobscot Bay, he knows they were farmers before they became fishermen. Fishing goes back at least two generations in the Hardie family and the sea is assuredly in Pearl's soul. He grew up on Bear Island, where his father was caretaker, and at the age of nine began lobstering from his own outboard with 25 traps. During his teens, he worked sporadically in Deer Isle's grocery store, but keptgoing back to fishing. It was not until he was about 19 that he bought his own 28-foot lobster boat and finally came to terms with his heritage. He now takes enormous pride in his honorable trade. His passion for his profession is so evident that his wife, Diane, insists she would "be history if he were forced to choose between me and fishing." Pearl now lobsters in the summer (with 700 traps!) and scallops in the winter. His face and demeanor reveal his strength of character and love for his work. And his philosophy is succinct: "Never stay home because of fog. If you don't go, you'll be home all summer."

Pearl told us that his father and uncle were the men he most admired. Both were lobstermen afflicted with a degenerative condition that forced them literally to crawl from their boats up the docks to waiting vehicles. It is their examples of courage that enable Pearl to meet frigid February mornings with an enthusiasm that belies the inherent dangers and discomforts. He might paraphrase his philosophy to accommodate the scalloping season: "Never stay home because of snow. If you don't go, you'll be home all winter." —*Jean and Dud Hendrick*

GRILLED SEA SCALLOPS WITH
LIME CHERVIL CHARDONNAY SAUCE

Serves 6

The refreshing citrus flavor of the sauce balances the rich smokiness of the grilled scallops. This sauce is also good on pasta, such as black pepper fettuccine. The cooking time of these scallops will vary depending on their size. Grill the scallops until just opaque or they will become tough and chewy. If grilling is not possible, the scallops can be broiled in the oven.

2 pounds sea scallops,
   side muscle removed
3 tablespoons olive oil
Salt and pepper

SAUCE
2 shallots, finely diced
Juice and grated zest of 2 limes

1 cup Chardonnay or other dry white
   wine
2 tablespoons chopped fresh chervil
6 ounces unsalted butter, softened
Salt and pepper
Chopped fresh parsley for garnish

1. Place the scallops on skewers and brush with the olive oil. Season with salt and pepper and let stand at room temperature for 1 hour.
2. Prepare a charcoal grill.
3. *Prepare the sauce:* Place the shallots, lime juice, lime zest, and wine in a small saucepan. Bring to a simmer and cook until reduced to 2 tablespoons. Stir in the chervil; reduce the heat to low and slowly whisk in the butter a few pieces at a time. Do not allow the sauce to boil. Season lightly with salt and pepper and set aside in a warm place.
4. Grill the scallops quickly over a hot fire just until done. Remove the scallops from the skewers and divide among warm serving plates. Spoon 1 to 2 tablespoons of the sauce over each portion. Serve sprinkled with chopped parsley.

GRILLED RAINBOW TROUT WITH BRAISED CABBAGE, TOMATO-SWEET PEPPER RELISH, AND BALSAMIC VINEGAR GLAZE

Serves 6

Most people eat not only with their taste buds but with their eyes. The combination of colors and textures in this delicious dish is visually appealing. Light and easy to prepare, it makes a good midsummer meal. The relish and balsamic vinegar glaze can be prepared ahead of time. The glaze must be warmed slightly before serving. You can substitute halibut, striped bass, cod, or any other firm white-fleshed fish for the trout.

RELISH
4 tomatoes, peeled, seeded, and
  chopped
½ yellow bell pepper, finely diced
½ green bell pepper, finely diced
1 jalapeño pepper, finely diced
2 shallots, finely diced
6 tablespoons cider vinegar
½ cup sugar
Pinch each of ground cinnamon,
  ground cloves, ground mustard,
  ground coriander, ground ginger,
  and ground black pepper

GLAZE
1 cup balsamic vinegar
¼ cup dry red wine

4 tablespoons olive oil
1 leek, white part only, thinly sliced
1 small Savoy cabbage, thinly sliced
1 tablespoon chopped fresh thyme
  plus 6 sprigs for garnish
Salt and pepper
6 rainbow trout (10 ounces each),
  skinned and boned

1. *Prepare the relish:* Combine all the relish ingredients in a large saucepan. Bring to a boil; reduce the heat and gently simmer until the mixture thickens, about 20 to 30 minutes. Set aside to cool.
2. *Prepare the glaze:* In a small saucepan over medium heat, combine the vinegar and wine; cook until reduced to 2 tablespoons. It should be the consistency of light syrup. Cover and set aside in a warm place.
3. Prepare a charcoal grill.
4. Heat 2 tablespoons of the olive oil in a large sauté pan over medium heat. Add the leek and sauté for 1 minute. Add the cabbage and chopped thyme; reduce the heat to low and continue to cook, covered, for 5 minutes, stirring occasionally. Season with salt and pepper and set aside in a warm place.
5. Brush the trout with the remaining 2 tablespoons olive oil and season with salt and pepper. Grill the trout for 1 minute per side.
6. Drizzle each serving plate with 1 teaspoon of the glaze. Place a portion of the cabbage mixture in the center of each plate. Top with a grilled trout, and place 1 to 2 tablespoons of the relish on top of the fish. Garnish with a sprig of thyme and serve.

BOUILLABAISSE

Serves 8

This is one of very few elegant entrées that you can eat with your hands. It is a festive and satisfying soup perfect for autumn when the variety of shellfish available is outstanding. Remember that the bouillabaisse will be only as good as its ingredients, so buy the freshest seafood available. Monkfish, hake, haddock, striped bass, mako shark, or cod would all work well in this dish. For convenience, the roasted peppers, lobster stock, and seafood-vegetable mixture (through step 5) can be prepared ahead of time.

LOBSTER STOCK:
2 lobsters (1½ pounds each)
2 tablespoons olive oil
1 onion, finely diced
1 carrot, finely diced
1 stalk celery, finely diced
1 clove garlic, minced
2 tablespoons chopped fresh
  parsley
1 sprig fresh thyme
1 tablespoon chopped fresh
  chervil
1 bay leaf
1 cup dry white wine
6 cups water
1 tablespoon lemon juice

SEAFOOD AND VEGETABLES:
2 red bell peppers
2 tablespoons olive oil
2 leeks, white part only, finely diced
1 bulb fennel, cored and finely diced
1 small onion, finely diced

3 cloves garlic, minced
1 teaspoon grated orange zest (about ½
  orange)
Pinch of saffron
5 tomatoes, peeled, seeded, and diced
½ cup dry white wine
1 tablespoon chopped fresh parsley
  plus more for garnish
1 bay leaf
2 tablespoons Pernod or other anise-
  flavored liqueur
Salt and pepper
24 littleneck clams, scrubbed and
  cleaned of any dirt
1 pound halibut fillet, cut into 2-inch
  pieces
16 sea scallops (about 1 pound), side
  muscle removed
8 large Gulf shrimp, peeled and deveined

Chopped fresh chives for garnish

French bread for accompaniment

1. Place the bell peppers over a charcoal fire or gas flame or under the broiler. Roast until the skin is uniformly charred, turning the peppers as needed. Place the peppers in a plastic bag, seal tightly, and allow to steam for 30 minutes. Remove the peppers from the bag, peel away the skin, cut the peppers in half, and discard the seeds and stems. Finely dice the peppers and set aside.

2. *Prepare the lobsters and stock:* Steam the lobsters for 10 minutes; remove from heat and allow to cool.

3. Remove the lobster meat from the tail and claw sections; reserve the shells. Dice the meat and set aside. Split the body section of the lobster in half and discard the green tomalley, the sand sac behind the eyes, and the gill tissues. Rinse the

body section under cold water. Chop the body and the tail and claw shells into small pieces for the stock.

4. Heat the olive oil in a 6-quart stockpot over medium-high heat. Add the onion, carrot, celery, and garlic; cook until the vegetables are lightly browned, 8 to 10 minutes, stirring occasionally. Add the lobster shells along with the remaining stock ingredients. Bring to a boil, reduce the heat, and slowly simmer the stock for 30 minutes.

5. Strain the stock through cheesecloth or a fine mesh strainer. Set aside 4 cups of the stock for the bouillabaisse. Reserve any leftover stock for another use.

6. *Prepare the seafood and vegetables:* Heat the olive oil in a large stockpot over medium-high heat. Add the leek, fennel, onion, and garlic; sauté for 4 to 5 minutes. Stir in the roasted bell pepper, orange zest, saffron, tomato, wine, the 1 tablespoon parsley, the bay leaf, Pernod, and reserved 4 cups lobster stock. Bring to a boil and season with salt and pepper. Reduce the heat and gently simmer for 10 minutes.

7. Add the clams to the pot; cover and cook just until the clams start to open, about 2 minutes. Add the halibut, scallops, and shrimp; cook just until the seafood is done, about 2 to 3 minutes. Add the reserved lobster meat and continue to cook for 30 seconds.

8. Transfer the seafood to serving bowls. Check the seasoning of the broth and ladle it over the seafood. Garnish with the parsley and chives and serve with French bread.

CONFIT OF DUCK WITH ROASTED VEGETABLES AND PLUMS

Serves 4

Confit is a classic French method of preserving meats, usually duck and goose, in their rendered fat. The leg and thigh are typically used to make confit. Although it takes considerable time and advance preparation to make confit, once made it is convenient to have on hand as a quick meal. It keeps in the refrigerator for up to 2 months and takes only a few minutes to reheat. It can be reheated in the oven or on a grill, or pan-fried in its own fat until the skin is browned and crisp.

CONFIT
½ cup kosher salt
2 bay leaves, crushed
1 tablespoon fennel seeds
1 tablespoon dried thyme
1 tablespoon cracked black pepper
4 duck legs, including thighs
2 quarts duck fat

ROASTED VEGETABLES
1 onion, diced
2 carrots, diced
1 stalk celery, diced
1 yellow squash, diced
1 red bell pepper, diced
1 jalapeño pepper, minced
1 clove garlic, minced
3 plums, pitted and sliced
1 tablespoon chopped fresh ginger
1 teaspoon curry powder
1 tablespoon chopped fresh cilantro
1 tablespoon chopped fresh parsley
Salt and pepper

1. *Prepare the confit:* Mix together the salt, bay leaves, fennel, thyme, and black pepper in a small bowl. Rub the duck legs with the mixture and refrigerate overnight.
2. Preheat the oven to 300°.
3. Remove the duck from the refrigerator and wipe away the salt mixture. Melt the duck fat in a deep roasting pan. Place the duck in the fat, making sure that the duck is completely covered with fat. Cover the pan with aluminum foil and bake for 2 hours.
4. Remove the pan from the oven. Remove the duck from the fat and set aside. Strain the fat through cheesecloth or a fine mesh strainer, leaving behind any sediment on the bottom of the pan. Only the fat is used to preserve the duck.
5. Place the duck in a deep stainless steel pan or an earthenware container. Reserve 2 tablespoons of the duck fat, then pour the rest of the fat over the duck to completely cover it. Allow to cool thoroughly, then cover the pan and refrigerate for at least 1 week or up to 2 months. The duck must remain completely covered with fat while being stored.
6. *Final preparation:* Preheat the oven heat to 350°.
7. *Prepare the roasted vegetables:* Combine the vegetables, plums, ginger, and curry powder in a bowl. Melt the reserved 2 tablespoons duck fat. Pour the fat over the

vegetables and stir to coat. Place the mixture in a roasting pan and roast until the vegetables are soft, about 20 to 25 minutes, stirring occasionally.

8. Meanwhile, reheat the duck. Transfer the duck to a roasting pan and bake at 350° for 15 minutes.

9. Remove the roasted vegetable mixture from the oven and stir in the cilantro and parsley. Season with salt and pepper.

10. Place the roasted vegetable mixture in the center of each serving plate. Top with the duck and serve.

WOOD-GRILLED QUAIL WITH SUN-DRIED CHERRY SAUCE AND SWISS CHARD

Serves 4

This is a wonderful combination of smoky, sweet, and tart flavors. Be careful not to overcook the quail because the flesh will dry out. This dish would also make an excellent first course; serve 1 quail per person.

MARINADE	
¾ cup dry red wine	8 boneless quail
1 teaspoon fennel seeds	6 tablespoons unsalted butter, softened
¼ cup orange juice	Salt and pepper
2 shallots, finely diced	1 bunch Swiss chard
1 carrot, finely diced	2 carrots, diced
½ cup sun-dried cherries	1 strip bacon, diced
2 tablespoons crème de cassis	2 shallots, diced
1 tablespoon chopped fresh parsley	1 clove garlic, minced
¼ cup olive oil	1 tablespoon balsamic vinegar
	Ground black pepper

1. *Prepare the marinade:* Combine all the marinade ingredients in a stainless steel or glass bowl. Add the quail and marinate for 6 hours.
2. Prepare a charcoal fire with fruitwood, preferably cherry.
3. Remove the quail from the marinade and wipe off any excess marinade. Pour the marinade into a small saucepan; bring to a boil over medium-high heat. Reduce the heat and slowly simmer until the marinade is reduced to 2 to 3 tablespoons. Turn the heat to low and swirl in the butter, 1 tablespoon at a time. Do not allow the sauce to boil. Strain the sauce and season with salt and pepper. Set aside in a warm place.
4. Separate the Swiss chard stems from the leaves. Finely dice the stems; wash the leaves and roughly chop. Cook the stems and the carrot in boiling water for 2 minutes; drain and set aside with the chard leaves.
5. Cook the bacon in a skillet over medium heat until crisp. Add the shallots and garlic; cook for 2 to 3 minutes. Stir in the chard leaves, stems, and carrot; cook until the chard wilts, about 3 to 4 minutes, stirring occasionally.
6. Stir in the vinegar. Season with black pepper and cook for 1 minute. Remove from the heat and keep warm.
7. Grill the quail until nicely browned, about 2 to 3 minutes per side.
8. Place a portion of the chard mixture in the center of each serving plate. Arrange the quail around it and spoon some of the sauce over the quail. Serve immediately.

GRILLED BREAST OF CHICKEN WITH WILD MUSHROOMS AND SORREL SAUCE

Serves 4

The tart, lemony flavor of the sorrel is a nice counterbalance to the richness of the mushrooms and the smokiness of the grilled chicken. Sorrel is an herb that is very easy to grow but expensive to buy. If sorrel is not available, watercress can be successfully substituted. For convenience, the chicken breast can be allowed to marinate overnight.

6 tablespoons olive oil
1 tablespoon lime juice (2 small limes)
Salt and pepper
4 boneless chicken breasts (6 ounces each)
2 shallots, finely diced
12 ounces fresh mushrooms (any combination of oyster, shiitake, chanterelle, portabello, or porcini mushrooms), chopped
1 tablespoon chopped fresh thyme plus 4 sprigs for garnish

1 tablespoon chopped fresh parsley
¼ cup port wine
1 small leek, white part only, finely diced
2 cloves garlic, finely diced
3 cups tightly packed sorrel (2 to 3 ounces), washed, dried, and finely diced
¼ cup Chicken Stock (page 138)
8 tablespoons unsalted butter, softened

1. Whisk together 4 tablespoons of the olive oil and the lime juice in a small bowl. Season with salt and pepper and pour over the chicken breasts; cover and refrigerate for 8 hours. Remove from the refrigerator 1 hour before grilling.
2. Heat 1 tablespoon of the olive oil in a skillet over medium heat. Add the shallots and cook for 1 minute. Stir in the mushrooms and continue to cook until soft, about 5 to 6 minutes, stirring often. Stir in the chopped thyme, parsley, and port; season with salt and pepper and cook for 2 minutes. Remove from the heat and set aside in a warm place.
3. Heat the remaining 1 tablespoon olive oil in a large saucepan over medium heat. Add the leek and garlic; sauté for 2 to 3 minutes. Stir in the sorrel; reduce the heat to low, cover, and cook for 2 minutes. Add the stock; season with salt and pepper and cook uncovered for 2 minutes.
4. Remove from heat and purée in a blender. Strain back into the saucepan and, over low heat, swirl in the butter 1 tablespoon at a time. Do not allow the sauce to boil. Remove from heat and set aside in a warm place.
5. Prepare a charcoal grill. Grill the chicken over a medium-high fire for 2 to 3 minutes per side.
6. Portion the sauce in the center of each serving plate. Place the chicken on top of the sauce. Arrange the mushrooms on top and alongside the chicken. Serve garnished with a sprig of thyme.

CITRUS HERB-ROASTED
DEER ISLE FARM CHICKEN

Serves 4

The secret to this exceptionally moist chicken is the citrus herb butter under the breast skin and the constant basting. Free-range chickens are increasingly available in good supermarkets across the country. We find free-range chicken to be leaner, visually more appealing, and much more flavorful than other chicken. However, if free-range chickens are not available, regular roasting chicken may be substituted.

CITRUS HERB BUTTER
¼ pound unsalted butter, softened
1 tablespoon chopped fresh rosemary
1 tablespoon chopped fresh thyme
1 tablespoon chopped fresh parsley
2 cloves garlic, minced
Juice and grated zest of 1 lemon
Salt and pepper

1 free-range chicken (3½ to 4 pounds)
Salt and pepper
1 clove garlic, peeled
1 small onion, peeled and cut in half
2 tablespoons chopped fresh rosemary
2 tablespoons olive oil
1 cup Chicken Stock (page 138)

1. *Prepare the citrus herb butter:* Stir together the butter, herbs, garlic, and lemon juice and zest in a small bowl until well blended. Season with salt and pepper and set aside.
2. Preheat the oven to 400°.
3. Remove any excess fat from the chicken cavity. Rinse the chicken inside and out with cold water and dry with paper towels.
4. Lift up the breast skin and place the citrus herb butter between the breast meat and the skin. Spread the butter to evenly coat the breast.
5. Season the cavity with salt and pepper. Place the garlic, onion, and 1 tablespoon of the rosemary in the cavity. Truss the legs and fold the wings under the chicken. Place the chicken on a rack in a roasting pan. Brush the chicken legs with the olive oil and season with salt and pepper.
6. Roast the chicken for 1 hour and 15 minutes, basting every 20 minutes with the pan juices. Remove from the oven and allow to rest for 20 minutes.
7. Pour off and discard the fat from the roasting pan. Pour in the stock and add the remaining 1 tablespoon rosemary. Deglaze the pan over high heat.
8. Carve the chicken. Strain the pan juices and serve with the chicken.

Shiitake mushrooms, free-range chicken, and raspberries from Carl and Priscilla Woodward

After sowing his wild oats from Boston to Oklahoma, Carl Woodward returned to Deer Isle to become a real farmer. In the mid-1980s, he joined his mother, Priscilla, on the family-run Island Acres Farm—the only working farm on the island and one that has been tilled by their forebears since 1793. Through determination and experimentation, they have managed to grow raspberries on their rock-strewn hills and to produce free-range chickens, turkeys, and lambs that have graced the tables of island folks for years.

Today they have a small poultry processing plant and supply free-range chicken to area restaurants. They are also producing sausage that is highly acclaimed for its taste as well as for being a derivative of organic farming principles. Pilgrim's Inn has been a customer from the very beginning, and our guests will attest to the superiority of the Island Acres products.

In 1990, Carl found the energy and creative desire for yet another enterprise—cultivating shiitake mushrooms. From an initial experiment with 70 logs, the mushroom farm has grown to 20,000 logs, which are inoculated, tended, and set for a year before each one produces pounds of these delectable fungi. Throughout the season, they have become a staple, both fresh and dried, at the Inn.

As the market for mushrooms and free-range chickens continues to grow, Priscilla and Carl are optimistic about their business. We eagerly await the introduction of new products, knowing they will be fresh, wholesome, and chemical-free.

—Jean and Dud Hendrick

JEAN'S PAELLA

Serves 8

Jean would serve this delightful Spanish dish on Sundays, and it was so successful that the guests would not let her take it off the menu. It is well suited to large groups. You can vary the vegetables, meats, and seafood according to what is local and fresh. The shrimp, vegetable-sausage mixture, and chicken can be prepared in advance (through step 3) and refrigerated until needed. Paella *refers to the pan traditionally used to prepare this dish.*

1 pound medium shrimp, peeled, and deveined
1 tablespoon lemon juice
1 tablespoon chopped fresh oregano
2 tablespoons olive oil
Salt and pepper
¼ pound bacon, diced
1 onion, diced
1 green bell pepper, diced
3 cloves garlic, minced
1 pound chorizo or other smoked sausage, cooked and sliced
8 boneless, skinless chicken breasts (4 to 6 ounces each), cut in half
3 cups rice
6 cups Chicken Stock (page 138)

½ cup dry white wine
½ teaspoon saffron, crushed
1 teaspoon paprika
2 tablespoons chopped fresh cilantro
1 bay leaf
2 tablespoons chopped fresh oregano
1 tablespoon chopped fresh thyme
2 tomatoes, peeled, seeded, and chopped
1 cup peas
2 dozen mussels or clams, debearded and scrubbed
Chopped fresh parsley
2 lemons, quartered

1. Combine the shrimp, lemon juice, oregano, and olive oil in a bowl. Season with salt and pepper and toss together until the shrimp are well coated. Set aside.
2. Cook the bacon in a large skillet over medium heat until crisp. Add the onion, bell pepper, and garlic; cook until softened, about 5 minutes, stirring often. Stir in the sausage and cook 3 to 4 minutes longer. Remove the vegetables and sausage and set aside.
3. To the same skillet add the chicken and cook until lightly browned, about 1 to 2 minutes on each side. Remove from the skillet and set aside.
4. Preheat the oven to 350°.
5. Remove all but 1 tablespoon of fat from the skillet. Add the rice and stir to coat with the fat. Stir in the stock, wine, saffron, paprika, cilantro, bay leaf, oregano, thyme, and tomatoes; season with salt and pepper. Bring to a boil; reduce the heat to low and cook, stirring often, about 15 minutes. The rice will not yet be cooked through. Remove from heat and stir in the peas and vegetable-sausage mixture.
6. Transfer the mixture to a paella pan or a roasting pan. Bury the cooked chicken and shrimp in the rice. Push the mussels into the top of the rice and bake in the oven until the mussels open, about 15 to 20 minutes.
7. Serve hot, garnished with chopped parsley and lemon wedges.

GRILLED CURED LOIN OF PORK WITH BRAISED RASPBERRY CABBAGE

Serves 8

The brine tenderizes and imparts a cured-hamlike quality to the pork, which makes it moist and very flavorful. The loin may be roasted, smoked, or cut into medallions and sautéed. Remember when storing the pork that it must remain completely submerged in the brine and be covered tightly to prevent contamination.

½ cup kosher salt
¼ cup sugar
8 cups hot water
1 small onion, finely diced
2 cloves garlic, peeled
1 stalk celery, finely diced
1 carrot, finely diced
1 teaspoon mustard seeds
1 teaspoon black peppercorns
1 tablespoon fennel seeds
2 tablespoons chopped fresh parsley

1 bay leaf
2 tablespoons chopped fresh rosemary plus 8 sprigs for garnish
2 whole cloves
1 center-cut boneless pork loin (about 3 pounds), trimmed of all fat
5 tablespoons olive oil
2 shallots, finely diced
1 Savoy cabbage (about 2 pounds), tough outer leaves discarded, thinly sliced
Salt and pepper
¼ cup raspberry vinegar

1. Make a brine by whisking together the salt, sugar, and hot water in a large bowl until the salt and sugar dissolve. Stir in the onion, garlic, celery, carrot, mustard seeds, peppercorns, fennel, parsley, bay leaf, chopped rosemary, and cloves. Allow to cool.
2. Place the pork in the brine; cover and refrigerate for 48 hours.
3. Prepare a charcoal grill.
4. Remove the pork from the brine and pat dry with paper towels. Coat the pork with 3 tablespoons of the olive oil. Grill over a medium-low fire to an internal temperature of 145°. It should take 30 to 40 minutes. Remove from the grill and allow to stand for 15 minutes.
5. Heat the remaining 2 tablespoons olive oil in a large saucepan over medium-high heat. Add the shallots and cook for 1 minute. Add the cabbage and season with salt and pepper; cover, reduce the heat to low, and slowly braise for 10 minutes, stirring occasionally. Add the vinegar and cook for 5 minutes more.
6. Place a portion of the cabbage mixture on each serving plate. Carve the pork into thin slices and arrange on top of the cabbage. Garnish each plate with a sprig of rosemary and serve.

GRILLED MARINATED LEG OF LAMB

Serves 6

The grill will be hot while cooking the lamb, so you could also grill eggplant, leeks, asparagus, or rosemary potatoes to accompany this dish. The top round cut of the leg can be purchased from some butcher shops. It has very little fat and should be uniform in size for easy grilling. It will cost a little more per pound than buying a whole leg but will save you time trimming and will produce much less waste.

2 bulbs garlic	1 teaspoon cracked black pepper
8 tablespoons olive oil	1 tablespoon chopped fresh savory
1 boneless leg of lamb (4 to 5 pounds)	2 tablespoons balsamic vinegar
2 tablespoons chopped fresh rosemary	Grated zest of 1 orange
1 teaspoon salt	

1. Preheat the oven to 300°.
2. Rub the garlic with 2 tablespoons of the olive oil. Place in a small roasting pan, cover with aluminum foil, and bake for 1 hour. Remove from the oven and allow to cool for 30 minutes.
3. Cut a ½-inch slice off the top of each bulb and squeeze out the soft garlic. Set aside.
4. Trim the lamb of all fat, sinew, and membrane; cut into 3 or 4 pieces of uniform size.
5. In a small bowl, whisk together the roasted garlic, the remaining 6 tablespoons olive oil, the rosemary, salt, pepper, savory, vinegar, and orange zest. Pour the mixture over the lamb; cover and refrigerate overnight.
6. Remove the lamb from the refrigerator 30 minutes before grilling.
7. Prepare a charcoal grill. Grill the lamb over a medium-high fire to desired doneness, about 8 to 10 minutes per side for medium-rare.
8. Remove the lamb from the grill and allow to stand for 15 minutes. Carve into thin slices and serve.

GRILLED LOIN LAMB CHOPS WITH COUSCOUS, PLUM CHUTNEY, AND ROSEMARY OIL

Serves 6

The pure, refreshing flavor of the chutney is an ideal match for the grilled lamb and spicy couscous. For deliciously moist and tender lamb, serve the loin chops medium-rare.

½ cup olive oil
2 sprigs fresh rosemary plus 12
    sprigs for garnish
12 loin lamb chops (5 ounces each)
Salt and pepper

CHUTNEY
1 pound plums, pitted and finely diced
1 Granny Smith apple, peeled, cored,
    and finely diced
2 tablespoons dried currants or raisins
¾ cup apple cider
¼ cup firmly packed brown sugar
1 shallot, finely diced
1 teaspoon chopped fresh ginger

1 clove garlic, minced
1 tablespoon chopped fresh mint
Pinch of ground allspice
Pinch of cayenne pepper

COUSCOUS
½ green bell pepper, finely diced
1 scallion, finely diced
1 carrot, peeled and finely diced
2 cups Chicken Stock (page 138)
1 teaspoon curry powder
2 tablespoons chopped fresh parsley
2 tablespoons unsalted butter
Salt and pepper
1 cup couscous

1. Heat the olive oil and 2 sprigs of the rosemary in a small saucepan over medium heat until the rosemary starts to sizzle. Remove from heat and allow to steep for 1 hour.
2. Strain the oil and discard the rosemary. Coat the lamb chops with half of the rosemary oil and allow to marinate for 6 hours.
3. *Prepare the chutney:* Combine all the chutney ingredients in a saucepan and bring to a boil over medium-high heat. Reduce the heat and gently simmer until the mixture thickens, about 30 to 40 minutes. Remove from heat and set aside in a warm place.
4. Prepare a charcoal grill.
5. Season the lamb with salt and pepper and grill over a medium-high fire to desired doneness, about 3 to 4 minutes per side for medium-rare. Keep warm.
6. *Meanwhile, prepare the couscous:* Combine the vegetables, stock, curry powder, parsley, and butter in a saucepan. Season with salt and pepper and bring to a boil. Stir in the couscous; remove from heat, cover, and allow to stand for 5 minutes.
7. Place a portion of the couscous in the center of each serving plate. Place a portion of the chutney in the center of the couscous. Arrange 2 lamb chops alongside the couscous and drizzle a little rosemary oil over each chop. Garnish each plate with 2 sprigs of rosemary and serve.

HERB-CRUSTED TENDERLOIN OF BEEF WITH ROASTED BELL PEPPERS, SHIITAKE MUSHROOMS, LEEKS, AND BALSAMIC VINEGAR GLAZE

Serves 6

For convenience, other cuts of beef may be substituted; sirloin steak, top round, or flank steak, trimmed of all fat, can be successfully used. The cooking time of the meat will vary depending on which cut you select. The beef may be grilled instead of roasted, again with a slight change in the cooking time. The roasted bell peppers and the beef rubbed with the herb paste can be prepared in advance, then covered and refrigerated until needed.

2 red bell peppers	3 leeks, white part only, thinly sliced
3 cloves garlic, peeled and left whole, plus 2 cloves garlic, minced	1 pound fresh shiitake mushrooms, thinly sliced
3 tablespoons fennel seeds	1 tablespoon chopped fresh parsley
1 teaspoon salt	1 tablespoon chopped fresh thyme plus 6 sprigs fresh thyme
2 tablespoons whole black peppercorns	
3 tablespoons olive oil	Salt and pepper
2 tablespoons chopped fresh rosemary	1 cup balsamic vinegar
1 center-cut beef tenderloin (about 2 pounds), well trimmed	¼ cup dry red wine

1. Place the bell peppers over a charcoal fire or gas flame or under the broiler. Roast until the skin is uniformly charred, turning the peppers as needed. Place the peppers in a plastic bag, seal tightly, and allow to steam for 30 minutes. Remove the peppers from the bag, peel away the skin, cut the peppers in half, and discard the seeds and stems. Cut the peppers into thin strips and set aside.

2. Preheat the oven to 375°.

3. In a mortar and pestle or coffee grinder, crush the 3 whole cloves garlic, fennel seeds, salt, and peppercorns to make a paste. Stir in 2 tablespoons of the olive oil and the rosemary.

4. Rub the paste over the beef. Set the meat in a roasting pan with a rack and roast to desired doneness, about 45 to 50 minutes for medium-rare. Remove from the oven and let stand for 15 minutes.

5. Meanwhile, heat the remaining 1 tablespoon olive oil in a large sauté pan over medium-high heat. Add the minced garlic and cook just until it starts to brown. Add the leek and mushrooms; reduce the heat to medium and sauté until the vegetables are soft, about 4 to 5 minutes. Stir in the parsley, chopped thyme, and roasted bell pepper strips; cook for 1 minute. Season with salt and pepper and set aside in a warm place.

6. In a small saucepan simmer the vinegar and wine over medium heat until reduced to a light syrupy consistency. You should have 2 to 3 tablespoons of glaze. Remove from the heat, cover with plastic wrap, and set aside in a warm place.

7. Cut the beef into ½-inch-thick slices. Using a spoon, drizzle about 2 teaspoons of the balsamic glaze on each serving plate. Place a portion of the mushroom mixture in the center of each plate. Arrange the beef slices alongside the mushroom mixture. Serve garnished with a sprig of thyme.

VENISON STEW WITH SPINACH AND ROOT VEGETABLES

Serves 6

This hearty dish is well suited to cool autumn days or cold winter ones. Venison is a lean, tender red meat that is rich and full flavored. Its health attributes are many: it is high in protein and low in fat and has about half the calories of lamb, beef, or pork. It is also an easily digestible and good source of iron.

4 cups Beef Stock (page 139)
1 ounce dried shiitake mushrooms
2 tablespoons all-purpose flour
Salt and pepper
1 venison leg (1½ pounds), trimmed of fat, cut into ¾-inch pieces
3 tablespoons olive oil
1 small leek, white part only, finely diced
2 shallots, finely diced
1 clove garlic, minced
¼ cup dry red wine
1 tomato, peeled, seeded, and diced

1 bay leaf
1 tablespoon chopped fresh parsley
1 tablespoon chopped fresh thyme
1 tablespoon chopped fresh savory
2 carrots, peeled and diced
1 russet potato, peeled and cut into ½-inch cubes
1 parsnip, peeled and diced
1 small rutabaga, peeled and diced
12 ounces spinach, stems removed, leaves washed and roughly chopped

1. Bring 1 cup of the stock to a boil in a small saucepan. Remove from heat and add the dried mushrooms. Allow the mushrooms to soak for 30 minutes.
2. Drain the mushrooms and reserve the liquid. Chop the mushrooms and set aside.
3. Season the flour with salt and pepper. Dredge the venison pieces in the flour.
4. Heat 2 tablespoons of the olive oil in a large skillet over medium-high heat. Add the venison and cook until browned on all sides. Remove the venison and set aside.
5. In the same skillet, heat the remaining 1 tablespoon olive oil over medium-high heat. Add the leek, shallots, and garlic; sauté for 5 minutes. Add the wine and cook for 3 to 4 minutes more.
6. Add the remaining 3 cups beef stock, the tomato, bay leaf, herbs, cooked venison, and reserved mushrooms and liquid. Bring to a boil; reduce heat to low, partially cover, and cook for 1 hour and 15 minutes.
7. Add the carrot, potato, parsnip, and rutabaga to the pot; cook until the vegetables and venison are tender, about 20 minutes. Season with salt and pepper.
8. Stir in the spinach just before serving.

DESSERTS

APPLE CRISP WITH ROSEMARY ICE CREAM

Serves 6

We make this crisp often in autumn when the apples on the island are in season and full of flavor. Rosemary and apples work beautifully together. For a more pronounced rosemary flavor, add a few more sprigs of rosemary and allow the mixture to steep longer. For a variation using the same ingredients, sauté the apples in rosemary butter and serve with cinnamon ice cream.

ROSEMARY ICE CREAM
2 sprigs fresh rosemary
1 cup half-and-half
2 cups heavy cream
1 cup granulated sugar
6 egg yolks
Few drops vanilla extract

APPLE CRISP
5 apples (Granny Smith, Gravenstein, or Winesap)
10 tablespoons unsalted butter
½ teaspoon ground cinnamon
¾ cup all-purpose flour
½ cup granulated sugar
½ cup firmly packed brown sugar

1. *Prepare the ice cream:* Place the rosemary, half-and-half, heavy cream, and sugar in a medium saucepan; bring just to a simmer, stirring occasionally. Remove from the heat and allow to steep for 30 minutes. Remove and discard the rosemary.
2. Whisk together the egg yolks and vanilla in a medium bowl just until combined. Slowly whisk in the cream mixture.
3. Pour everything back into the saucepan and cook over medium-low heat just until the mixture starts to thicken, stirring constantly. Strain into another bowl and chill completely. Freeze in an ice cream maker according to the manufacturer's instructions.
4. *Prepare the apple crisp:* Preheat the oven to 350°. Peel and core the apples; cut into 2-inch pieces.
5. Heat 2 tablespoons of the butter in a large skillet over medium-high heat. Add the apples and sprinkle with the cinnamon. Sauté for 3 to 4 minutes, stirring occasionally. Transfer to a baking dish.
6. Combine the flour and sugars in a bowl. With your fingertips or a pastry blender, work in the remaining 8 tablespoons butter until the mixture looks crumbly.
7. Sprinkle an even layer of the sugar mixture over the apples. Bake until the apples are tender and the top is lightly browned, about 30 to 40 minutes. Serve warm with the ice cream.

MACADAMIA PEACH CRISP

Serves 10

This is a perfect dessert for a cool summer night in Maine, especially when domestic peaches are in season and full of flavor. Serve slightly warm with ice cream or a pitcher of chilled heavy cream, or eat it cold for breakfast. Avoid hard green peaches; choose firm, ripe peaches that have a creamy color. A red color does not necessarily indicate ripeness.

8 firm, ripe peaches
1 tablespoon cornstarch
¾ cup plus 2 tablespoons sugar
1 cup all-purpose flour

Pinch of ground nutmeg
¼ pound unsalted butter
1 cup macadamia nuts (about 4 ounces), toasted and finely chopped

1. Preheat the oven to 350°.
2. Wash the peaches and pat dry. Slice around the seam and twist in half. Lift or cut out the pit, then cut the peaches into 2-inch pieces.
3. Combine the cornstarch and the 2 tablespoons sugar. Add the peaches and toss to coat. Place in a baking dish.
4. Combine the flour, the ¾ cup sugar, and the nutmeg in a bowl. Cut in the butter with your fingertips or a pastry blender until the mixture is crumbly.
5. Scatter the nuts evenly over the peaches, then sprinkle the crisp with the flour mixture. Bake until the top is light brown and the peaches are soft, about 45 minutes. Serve warm or at room temperature.

ALMOND MERINGUE TORTE WITH MOCHA BUTTERCREAM

Serves 10 to 12

This delicate, light, sweet torte has a wonderful almond-coffee flavor. The meringue shells and buttercream can be prepared ahead of time. Place the meringue shells in an airtight container and store at room temperature. Cover the buttercream with plastic wrap and store at room temperature until needed.

MERINGUE
1 cup sugar
½ teaspoon vanilla extract
2 cups sliced almonds (about
    6 ounces), toasted
1½ tablespoons cornstarch
6 egg whites, at room temperature
Pinch of cream of tartar

BUTTERCREAM
1 cup sugar
¼ cup water

Whites from 5 large eggs
½ teaspoon cream of tartar
1 pound butter, softened
2 tablespoons coffee liqueur
4 ounces bittersweet chocolate, melted
1 tablespoon Grand Marnier

GARNISH
1 cup sliced almonds (about 3 ounces),
    toasted
Shaved chocolate
Confectioners' sugar for sprinkling

1. Preheat the oven to 225°.
2. *Prepare the meringue:* Place ½ cup of the sugar, the vanilla, almonds, and cornstarch in a food processor and process until finely ground. Set aside.
3. In a double boiler combine the egg whites, the remaining ½ cup sugar, and the cream of tartar. Heat until the sugar is dissolved, stirring constantly. Transfer the mixture to a bowl of an electric mixer; using a whip attachment, beat to stiff peaks. Gently fold in the almond mixture.
4. Line 3 baking pans with parchment paper and trace a 9-inch circle on each. Spread the meringue mixture evenly on the circles. Bake the meringues until they are pale brown, about 1 to 1½ hours. Gently lift the meringues onto wire racks to cool.
5. *Meanwhile, prepare the buttercream:* Combine ¾ cup of the sugar and the water in a small saucepan. Cook over medium heat until the mixture reaches 234° on a candy thermometer.
6. Meanwhile, beat the egg whites in a bowl of an electric mixer until foamy. Slowly add the remaining ¼ cup sugar and the cream of tartar; continue to beat until stiff peaks form. With the mixer on medium-high speed, slowly and carefully pour the hot sugar syrup in a thin, steady stream between the side of the bowl and the beaters. Take care not to pour the syrup on the whip or it will splatter. Reduce the speed to low and beat until the mixture has cooled.
7. With the mixer on medium-high speed, add the butter 1 tablespoon at a time; beat until the mixture is smooth. Reduce the speed to low and add the coffee liqueur, chocolate, and Grand Marnier.

8. Place 1 meringue shell on a cake plate and spread some of the buttercream over the top. Lay another meringue shell on top and spread with buttercream. Top with the remaining meringue shell. Spread buttercream onto the sides and top of the torte. Press the toasted almonds onto the sides, and sprinkle the top with shaved chocolate. Refrigerate for 1 hour. Before serving, sprinkle confectioners' sugar over the chocolate.

REBEKAH'S GRANDMOTHER'S SOUR CREAM POUND CAKE

Serves 12 to 16

½ pound unsalted butter
3 cups sugar
6 eggs
3 cups cake flour, sifted
¼ teaspoon baking soda
1 cup sour cream

Fresh berries for accompaniment
Whipped cream flavored with Grand
    Marnier for accompaniment

1. Preheat the oven to 275°. Grease and lightly flour an angel food cake pan.
2. Using an electric mixer with a paddle attachment, cream the butter until light and fluffy. Add the sugar slowly and continue to beat until the mixture is again light and fluffy. Add the eggs one at a time until they are thoroughly incorporated.
3. Combine the flour and baking soda; add, alternating with the sour cream, to the egg mixture, scraping down the sides of the bowl when necessary.
4. Pour the batter into the prepared cake pan. Bake for 2 hours without peeking. If you must peek, wait until the last 15 minutes; this cake is sensitive. Serve with fresh berries and whipped cream flavored with Grand Marnier.

CHOCOLATE MACADAMIA COCONUT TART

Serves 8 to 10

The less the pastry dough is processed or worked, the flakier the crust will be. The dough will be much easier to work with if it is made the day before. Wrap it tightly in plastic wrap before placing it in the refrigerator, and take it out of the refrigerator and let stand at room temperature for 1 hour before rolling it out. The prebaked tart shell may be prepared in advance, then covered with plastic wrap and left at room temperature until needed. The tart should be baked 3 to 4 hours before serving time.

TART DOUGH
5 ounces butter
3 tablespoons solid vegetable shortening
2 cups all-purpose flour
1 tablespoon granulated sugar
½ teaspoon salt
¼ to ½ cup ice water
1 egg white mixed with 1 teaspoon water

FILLING
1 cup firmly packed brown sugar
½ cup granulated sugar
¼ pound unsalted butter

2 tablespoons heavy cream
2 ounces unsweetened chocolate, cut into small pieces
1 tablespoon all-purpose flour
2 eggs
½ teaspoon vanilla extract
½ cup unsweetened coconut, toasted
1½ cups macadamia nuts (about 6 ounces), toasted and finely chopped

Whipped cream for garnish

1. *Prepare the tart dough:* Cut the butter and shortening into very small pieces; place in the freezer for 1 hour.
2. Place the flour, sugar, and salt in a food processor. Add the chilled butter and shortening; process to the consistency of coarse meal, about 30 seconds. With the motor running, slowly add just enough ice water until the dough starts to form a ball.
3. Remove the dough from the processor and gather into a ball. Press into a circle, cover with plastic wrap, and let stand at room temperature for 1 hour.
4. Roll out the dough on a floured worktable. Press it into a 10-inch tart pan with a removable bottom. Refrigerate for 1 hour.
5. Preheat the oven to 350°.
6. Line the tart shell with aluminum foil and fill it with pie weights or dried beans. Bake for 20 minutes. Remove the foil and weights, brush the bottom of the shell with the egg white mixture, and continue to bake until lightly browned, about 10 minutes. Remove from the oven and set aside.
7. *Prepare the filling:* Place the sugars, butter, and cream in a small saucepan. Cook over low heat until the sugars have dissolved and the butter has melted, about 3 to 4 minutes, stirring often.
8. Remove from heat and stir in the chocolate and flour, mixing well.

9. Beat the eggs with the extract just until combined; stir into the chocolate mixture until thoroughly combined. Stir in the coconut and nuts.

10. Pour the filling into the chilled tart shell and bake until set and lightly browned, about 30 to 40 minutes. Remove from the oven and let cool. Serve garnished with whipped cream.

PEAR CUSTARD TART

Serves 8 to 10

Comice pears have a subtle buttery flavor that works nicely in this tart. Other pears that are in season may be substituted for equally satisfying results. Avoid overly ripe pears; a firm, ripe pear is best for cooking. The flesh should give slightly when pressed firmly with a fingertip. Also, avoid any pears that are very green or bruised.

TART DOUGH
5 ounces butter
3 tablespoons solid vegetable
  shortening
2 cups all-purpose flour
1 tablespoon sugar
1 teaspoon grated lemon zest
½ teaspoon salt
¼ to ½ cup ice water
1 egg white mixed with
  1 teaspoon water

FILLING
¾ cup sugar
¼ cup water
1½ Comice pears, peeled, cored,
  and thinly sliced
3 eggs
1 cup heavy cream
1 teaspoon grated lemon zest
2 tablespoons lemon juice
2 tablespoons butter, melted
2 tablespoons pear liqueur

Whipped cream for garnish

1. *Prepare the tart dough:* Cut the butter and shortening into very small pieces; place in the freezer for 1 hour.
2. Place the flour, sugar, lemon zest, and salt in a food processor. Add the chilled butter and shortening; process to the consistency of coarse meal, about 1 minute. With the motor running, slowly add just enough ice water until the dough starts to form a ball.
3. Remove the dough from the processor and gather into a ball. Press into a circle, cover with plastic wrap, and let stand at room temperature for 1 hour.
4. Roll out the dough on a floured worktable. Press it into a 10-inch tart pan with a removable bottom. Refrigerate for 1 hour.
5. Preheat the oven to 400°.
6. Line the tart shell with aluminum foil and fill it with pie weights or dried beans. Bake for 20 minutes. Remove the foil and weights, brush the bottom of the shell with the egg white mixture, and continue to bake until lightly browned, about 10 minutes. Remove from the oven and set aside.
7. *Prepare the filling:* Combine the sugar and water in a saucepan; cook over medium-high heat until the sugar has dissolved, about 1 to 2 minutes. Add the pears; cover, reduce the heat to medium-low, and cook until soft, about 15 minutes. Remove the pan from the heat; drain the pears and let cool. Purée the pears in a food processor.
8. In a medium bowl lightly whisk together the eggs and cream. Whisk in the lemon zest and juice, butter, and pear liqueur. Add pear purée and stir until blended.
9. Pour the filling into the tart shell. Bake until the custard is set, about 20 to 30 minutes. Remove from the oven and let cool. Garnish with whipped cream.

RASPBERRY CHOCOLATE CHEESECAKE

Serves 12

Pouring the ganache cream over the top and sides of the cheesecake is a messy but fun job that gives the cake a smooth, glazed appearance. Make sure you have ample space for this step; the ganache will run onto the work surface. Leftover ganache will keep, covered, in the refrigerator for up to 2 weeks. Cut the cheesecake with a sharp knife that has been dipped in hot water and dried.

CHEESECAKE
2 containers (12 ounces each)
  cream cheese, softened
1½ cups sugar
4 eggs plus 2 egg yolks
1 teaspoon vanilla extract
½ teaspoon lemon extract
¼ cup heavy cream

¼ cup raspberry liqueur
1 pint fresh raspberries

CHOCOLATE GANACHE
¾ cup heavy cream
6 ounces bittersweet chocolate,
  broken into ½-inch pieces
1 tablespoon raspberry liqueur

1. Preheat the oven to 350°.
2. Place the cream cheese in a bowl of an electric mixer fitted with a paddle. Beat on high speed until smooth, about 3 to 4 minutes. Scrape down the sides of the bowl and slowly add the sugar. Beat until well combined.
3. With the mixer on medium speed, slowly add the whole eggs and yolks one at a time. Beat until blended, scraping down the bowl after each egg is added. Add the extracts, cream, and liqueur; beat until well blended.
4. Grease a 9- by 2-inch cake pan. Pour the batter into the prepared pan, then place the pan in a larger pan and fill with enough hot water to reach halfway up the sides of the cake pan. Bake for 1 hour and 15 minutes; the top should be lightly brown and risen slightly above the top of the pan.
5. Remove the cheesecake from the oven and the water. Let cool on a wire rack for 1 hour.
6. Unmold the cheesecake onto a serving plate; the browned top will be the bottom of the cheesecake. Refrigerate for 4 hours.
7. *Prepare the chocolate ganache:* Bring the cream to a boil in a small saucepan over medium-high heat. Remove from the heat and whisk in the chocolate until smooth. Stir in the liqueur.
8. Pour the warm ganache evenly over the top and sides of the chilled cheesecake. Use a spatula to spread the ganache and clean up the excess.
9. Arrange the raspberries on top of the cheesecake while the ganache is still warm. Refrigerate for 1 hour before serving.

Strawberries from Dud

The successful innkeeper must wear many hats and have at least a passing acquaintance with such things as plumbing, glad-handing, bartending, cooking, electricity, carpentry, gardening, and finance, to name a few.

As the years have accumulated, I've found that the chores to which I devote the majority of my time have changed. One of the interests I've been increasingly able to pursue, serving both me and the Inn well, is gardening. Working the soil is a soothing counterpoint to the pressures of innkeeping, and it allows me to accomplish something vital to our goal of always providing guests with fresh produce.

During the winter of 1995–1996, Jean and I enrolled in the University of Maine Extension Service's Master Gardening course. What a terrific resource! The curriculum, which emphasized organic gardening and concentrated on fruits and vegetables, armed us with the knowledge to expand our already considerable gardening efforts.

Generally, Jean has had the pleasure of dealing with the exotica, while, for the most part, I've been the potato guy, keeping our guests and more than a few Colorado potato beetles surfeited with Russets, Norlands, and Kennebecs. My success with the mundane potato, and the not-so-romantic squash, cucumbers, and tomatoes, had me evaluating other possibilities—strawberries! They are beautiful, nearly universally appreciated, hardy enough to tolerate our climate, and just labor-intensive enough to make it worth the challenge. Besides, strawberries would provide Terry with fruit for summer desserts. Beginning in the spring of 1995, I devoted 3,200 square feet to 375 Annapolis, Sparkle, and Earliglow plants, which have been relatively pest- and disease-resistant. They have more than met my expectations and have enhanced many meals at the Inn.   —*Dud Hendrick*

STRAWBERRY CREAM TART

Serves 8 to 10

This simple, light dessert is perfect in summer. Raspberries, blueberries, or blackberries can be successfully substituted for the strawberries or combined with them. The tart shell and the cream mousse can be prepared in advance; however, the tart should be assembled as close to serving time as possible.

TART DOUGH
- 5 ounces butter
- 3 tablespoons solid vegetable shortening
- 2 cups all-purpose flour
- 1 tablespoon sugar
- ½ teaspoon salt
- ¼ to ½ cup ice water
- 1 egg white mixed with 1 teaspoon water

CREAM MOUSSE:
- 3 ounces cream cheese, softened
- ¼ cup confectioners' sugar
- Few drops vanilla extract
- 2 teaspoons Grand Marnier
- ¾ cup heavy cream

- 1 pint fresh strawberries

1. *Prepare the tart dough:* Cut the butter and shortening into very small pieces and place in the freezer for 1 hour.
2. Place the flour, sugar, and salt in a food processor. Add the chilled butter and shortening; process to the consistency of coarse meal, about 30 seconds. With the motor running, slowly add just enough ice water until the dough starts to form a ball.
3. Remove the dough from the processor and gather into a ball. Press into a circle, cover with plastic wrap, and let stand at room temperature for 1 hour.
4. Roll out the dough on a floured worktable. Press it into a 10-inch tart pan with a removable bottom. Refrigerate for 1 hour.
5. Preheat the oven to 350°.
6. Line the tart shell with aluminum foil and fill it with pie weights or dried beans. Bake the shell for 20 minutes. Remove the foil and weights, brush the bottom of the shell with the egg white mixture, and continue to bake until lightly browned, 10 to 15 minutes. Remove from the oven and set aside.
7. *Prepare the cream mousse:* Place the cream cheese, confectioners' sugar, vanilla, and Grand Marnier in a food processor and process until smooth, about 2 to 3 minutes, scraping down the sides of the work bowl as needed. Transfer the mixture to a large bowl.
8. Whip the heavy cream to soft peaks; gently fold into the cream cheese mixture. Spread the mixture on the bottom of the tart shell and arrange the fresh strawberries on top. Serve immediately.

PECAN PUMPKIN CRÈME BRÛLÉE TART

Serves 8

This dessert, a favorite at Pilgrim's Inn, combines two classics: crème brûlée and pumpkin pie. When caramelizing the tart under the broiler, it may be necessary to cover the edge of the tart shell with a small strip of aluminum foil to avoid burning the crust. Also, rotate the tart once or twice while caramelizing so the sugar browns evenly.

TART DOUGH
5 ounces unsalted butter
3 tablespoons solid vegetable
  shortening
2 cups all-purpose flour
½ cup pecan pieces (about 2 ounces),
  toasted
1 tablespoon granulated sugar
½ teaspoon salt
¼ to ½ cup ice water
1 egg white mixed with 1 teaspoon water

¼ cup firmly packed brown sugar

FILLING
2 cups heavy cream
8 egg yolks
¾ cup granulated sugar
1 cup pumpkin purée
Few drops vanilla extract
Pinch each of ground cinnamon
  and allspice

Whipped cream for garnish

1. *Prepare the tart dough:* Cut the butter and shortening into very small pieces; place in the freezer for 1 hour.

2. Place the flour, pecans, sugar, and salt in a food processor and process for 1 minute. Add the chilled butter and shortening; process to the consistency of coarse meal, about 30 seconds. With the motor running, slowly add just enough water until the dough starts to form a ball.

3. Remove the dough from the processor and gather into a ball. Press into a circle, cover with plastic wrap, and let stand at room temperature for 1 hour.

4. Roll out the dough on a floured worktable. Press it into a 10-inch tart pan with a removable bottom. Refrigerate for 1 hour.

5. Preheat the oven to 350°.

6. Place the brown sugar on a baking pan and bake for 10 minutes. Remove from the oven and let dry at room temperature.

7. *Prepare the filling:* Warm the cream in a small saucepan over medium heat.

8. Combine the egg yolks and granulated sugar in a large bowl. Slowly whisk in the cream. Stir in the pumpkin, vanilla, and spices; mix until well blended. Set aside.

9. Line the tart shell with aluminum foil and fill with pie weights or dried beans. Bake for 20 minutes. Remove the foil and weights, brush the bottom of the shell with the egg white mixture, and continue to bake until lightly browned, about 10 minutes.

10. Pour the filling into the tart shell. Bake until set, about 20 to 25 minutes. Remove from the oven and let cool at room temperature for 1 hour, then refrigerate for 2 hours.

11. Sieve an even layer of the dried brown sugar over the chilled tart. Place the tart under the broiler to caramelize the sugar. Serve garnished with whipped cream.

BLUEBERRY ALMOND TORTE

Serves 8

This updated classic substitutes blueberry jam for raspberry jam in the filling, and almonds for hazelnuts in the crust. Use the best jam you can find; it makes a world of difference.

8 ounces unsalted butter, softened
1 cup sugar
3 egg yolks
1½ cups all-purpose flour
½ teaspoon baking powder

½ teaspoon salt
1 tablespoon lemon zest
1⅓ cup ground almonds
1 cup blueberry jam

1. Sift the cake flour, baking powder, and salt into a bowl. Stir in the almonds and lemon.
2. Cream the butter and sugar in a mixing bowl until smooth and well blended.
3. Add the egg yolks one at a time, beating well after each addition.
4. Slowly add the dry ingredients and beat until well combined. Remove from the mixer, gather the dough into a ball, cover with plastic wrap and refrigerate for 1 hour.
5. Remove dough from the refrigerator and cut off ⅓ of the dough and return it to the refrigerator.
6. Roll out the remaining dough into an 11-inch circle, dusting with flour when necessary to prevent sticking. Place in a 9-inch tart pan with a removable bottom.
7. Spread the blueberry jam evenly over the bottom of the shell.
8. Remove the reserved dough from the refrigerator and roll out into a 9-inch circle. Cut the circle into ¾-inch strips and, using a spatula, carefully place half of the strips evenly over the top of the jam.
9. Place the remaining strips diagonally over the first strips, creating a lattice pattern. Press the strips to the edge of the pan and trim to fit.
10. Place the torte in the refrigerator for 1 hour.
11. Preheat oven to 375°.
12. Bake for 30–40 minutes until the top is lightly browned.
13. Remove from oven and cool completely. Serve with lightly sweetened whipped cream or Cinnamon Cognac Ice Cream (page 135).

CHOCOLATE CRÈME BRÛLÉE
WITH HAZELNUT PRALINE

Serves 8

In this dessert the delicious chocolate-flavored custard is topped with a crunchy layer of hazelnuts. The crème brûlée will keep for 2 to 3 days in the refrigerator; the praline will keep for weeks stored in a glass container in the refrigerator.

PRALINE

¾ cup sugar

¼ cup water

1 cup hazelnuts (about 5 ounces),
    toasted and coarsely chopped

CRÈME BRÛLÉE

2 cups heavy cream

1 cup milk

5 ounces bittersweet chocolate,
    cut into small pieces

½ cup sugar

7 extra large egg yolks

1. *Prepare the praline:* In a small saucepan stir together the sugar and water and bring to boil. Reduce the heat to medium and cook until syrupy and golden brown. Remove the pan from the heat and stir in the chopped nuts.
2. Line a baking pan with parchment paper; oil the paper. Pour the nut mixture onto the paper and spread it quickly to a thin layer. Let cool.
3. Transfer the praline to a food processor and process until finely ground. Set aside.
4. Preheat the oven to 325°.
5. *Prepare the crème brûlée:* Heat the cream and milk in a saucepan over medium-high heat just until the mixture starts to boil. Remove from heat and stir in the chocolate; mix until smooth.
6. In a large bowl slowly whisk the sugar into the egg yolks until combined. Slowly whisk in the chocolate mixture.
7. Strain the mixture through a fine mesh strainer. Pour into eight 6-ounce ramekins. Place the ramekins in a shallow baking pan and pour enough hot water into the pan to reach halfway up the sides of the ramekins.
8. Bake until the custards are set, about 35 to 45 minutes. Remove the ramekins from the water and allow to cool, then cover and refrigerate for 8 hours.
9. Before serving, briefly warm the ramekins in a 325° oven. Remove from the oven and cover the top of each ramekin with a thin layer of the praline. Serve immediately.

ALMOND CAKE

Serves 12

Adapted from a recipe in Lindsey Shere's Chez Panisse Desserts, *this cake is light and moist and needs only a dusting of confectioners' sugar. If the cake starts to brown before it is done, gently lay a piece of aluminum foil over the top while the cake bakes. Also, when mixing the cake batter in the food processor, it is important that the processor bowl be regularly scraped down. This will help avoid lumps in the batter and visible white spots in the baked cake.*

ALMOND PASTE
1⅓ cups sliced almonds (about 4 ounces)
½ cup granulated sugar
¼ teaspoon almond extract
3 to 4 tablespoons water

CAKE BATTER
1¼ cups granulated sugar
10 ounces unsalted butter, softened

6 eggs
1 teaspoon vanilla extract
1 cup all-purpose flour
1½ teaspoons baking powder
Pinch of salt

Confectioners' sugar for dusting

1. Preheat the oven to 325°. Grease a 9-inch springform pan.
2. *Prepare the almond paste:* Place the almonds, sugar, and extract in a food processor. Process for 1 minute, scraping down the sides of the bowl when necessary. With the motor running, slowly add just enough water to form a paste. Remove the paste, weigh out 8 ounces (about ¾ cup), and set aside. Refrigerate any leftover paste for another use.
3. *Prepare the cake batter:* Place the sugar and reserved almond paste in the processor and process for 1 minute. Add the butter and process until well combined, scraping down the sides of the bowl when necessary. With the motor running, slowly add the eggs and extract; process just until combined.
4. Sift together the flour, baking powder, and salt. Add to the processor and process until thoroughly mixed, about 30 seconds.
5. Pour the batter into the prepared pan. Bake until a toothpick inserted in the center comes out clean, about 1 hour and 20 minutes. Remove from the oven and let cool. Before serving, dust the top of the cake with confectioners' sugar.

FROZEN LEMON SOUFFLÉ

Serves 12 to 16

This summer dessert is ideal for entertaining because it can be prepared several hours in advance. When adding the hot sugar syrup to the beaten egg yolks, pour the syrup in a steady stream between the side of the mixing bowl and the whip. If the syrup comes in contact with the whip, it will splatter on the side of the bowl and not mix in with the eggs. Macadamia nuts, which go well with lemon, may be substituted for the almonds. Another variation is to use lime instead of lemon and add chopped fresh mint leaves.

2 cups granulated sugar
1 cup water
10 eggs, at room temperature
¾ cup lemon juice
2 tablespoons rum
2 tablespoons unflavored gelatin

3 cups heavy cream
2 tablespoons confectioners' sugar
1 cup sliced almonds (about 3 ounces), toasted

Whipped cream for garnish

1. Combine 1½ cups of the granulated sugar and ¾ cup of the water in a small saucepan. Cook over medium heat until the mixture reaches 234° on a candy thermometer. It will be syrupy.
2. Meanwhile, separate the eggs. Place the yolks in a bowl of an electric mixer; using a whip attachment, beat on medium-high speed until thick and pale yellow. Increase the speed to high and slowly pour in the hot sugar syrup in a thin, steady stream. Reduce the speed to low and pour in the lemon juice and rum. Continue to beat on low speed until the mixture has cooled.
3. Meanwhile, pour the remaining ¼ cup water into a small saucepan and place over low heat. Sprinkle the gelatin over the water and cook until dissolved, stirring occasionally.
4. While beating the lemon mixture on medium speed, slowly pour in the gelatin mixture. Transfer to a large bowl and set aside.
5. Clean the mixing bowl and pour in the cream and confectioners' sugar; beat to soft peaks. Transfer to another bowl and set aside.
6. Clean the mixing bowl and add the egg whites. Whisk on medium speed until foamy. Slowly add the remaining ½ cup granulated sugar; increase the speed to high and whisk until soft peaks form. Set aside.
7. Place the bowl containing the lemon mixture in a bowl of ice water; stir the mixture constantly just until it starts to thicken. Remove from the ice water and gently fold in the whipped cream. Gently fold in the egg white mixture along with the almonds just until blended.
8. Lightly spoon the mixture into individual soufflé dishes or ramekins. Place in the freezer for 8 hours. Serve garnished with whipped cream.

WHITE CHOCOLATE ICE CREAM

Makes 1 quart

1 cup half-and-half
¾ cup sugar
6 egg yolks
8 ounces white chocolate,
   broken into ½-inch pieces

2 cups heavy cream
Few drops vanilla extract

1. Combine the half-and-half and sugar in a small saucepan; cook over medium heat until the sugar dissolves, stirring constantly with a wooden spoon.
2. In a medium bowl lightly beat the egg yolks. Slowly whisk in the hot half-and-half mixture. Return the mixture to the saucepan and cook over low heat just until the mixture starts to thicken, stirring constantly.
3. Strain the mixture and set aside to cool slightly.
4. Melt the chocolate in the top of a double boiler set over barely simmering water, stirring constantly. Slowly whisk in the egg mixture. The chocolate may form lumps; continue to whisk until smooth.
5. Stir in the cream and vanilla. Strain the mixture into a bowl and chill thoroughly.
6. Freeze in an ice cream maker according to the manufacturer's instructions. Place ice cream in the freezer until serving time.

CINNAMON COGNAC ICE CREAM

Makes 1 quart

1 cup milk
2 cups heavy cream
⅔ cup sugar

1 stick cinnamon
6 egg yolks
2 tablespoons Cognac

1. Combine the milk, cream, sugar, and cinnamon stick in a saucepan. Cook over medium heat until the sugar is dissolved, stirring constantly.
2. In a medium bowl lightly whisk the egg yolks. Pour in the hot cream mixture, then pour everything back into the saucepan and cook over medium-low heat just until the mixture starts to thicken, stirring constantly.
3. Strain the mixture into a bowl. Rinse the cinnamon stick and add it back to the mixture. Stir in the Cognac and chill thoroughly.
4. Remove and discard the cinnamon stick. Freeze the mixture in an ice cream maker according to the manufacturer's instructions. Place ice cream in the freezer until serving time.

HAZELNUT CASSIS ICE CREAM

Makes 1 quart

2 cups hazelnuts (about 10 ounces),
  toasted
1½ cups milk
⅔ cup sugar

2 cups heavy cream
6 egg yolks
Few drops vanilla extract
1 tablespoon crème de cassis

1. Finely grind the nuts in a food processor. Set aside ½ cup; place the remaining nuts in a small saucepan.
2. Add the milk to the pan and bring to a simmer. Remove from the heat and allow to steep for 30 minutes.
3. Strain and discard the nuts; return the milk to the saucepan.
4. Add the sugar and cream to the milk and bring to a simmer over medium heat, stirring constantly.
5. Place the egg yolks in a medium bowl and slowly whisk in the hot milk mixture. Pour the mixture back into the saucepan and cook over medium-low heat until the mixture has thickened, stirring constantly.
6. Strain the mixture into a bowl; stir in the vanilla and cassis. Chill thoroughly.
7. Freeze in an ice cream maker according to the manufacturer's instructions. Remove from the ice cream maker and fold in the reserved ½ cup ground nuts. Place in the freezer until serving time.

BASICS

CHICKEN STOCK

Makes about 7 cups

When preparing stock, always maintain it at a gentle simmer; allowing it to boil will produce a cloudy and less flavorful stock. For a more intensely flavored stock, use bone-in chicken thighs instead of the necks, backs, and wings. Use the leftover cooked thigh meat for salads or toss with pasta. For an even more intense, rich flavor, repeat the stock preparation using chicken stock instead of water. Also, some cooks, in making stocks, use leftover kitchen scraps, such as onion skins, carrot scrapings, and other vegetable trimmings. Remember that a stock made with kitchen scraps will taste like kitchen scraps, so use only the freshest ingredients. This stock will keep for 3 to 4 days in the refrigerator or up to 2 months in the freezer. When freezing the stock, allow room for it to expand in its container.

2 tablespoons vegetable oil
3 pounds chicken bones, necks, backs, and wings
1 onion, chopped
1 carrot, chopped
1 stalk celery, chopped

12 cups cold water
1 bay leaf
4 sprigs fresh parsley
2 sprigs fresh thyme
2 cloves garlic, peeled

1. Preheat the oven to 375°.
2. Cover the bottom of a roasting pan with the vegetable oil. Place the chicken, onion, carrot, and celery in the pan; stir to coat with the oil. Roast until the chicken and vegetables are well browned, about 40 minutes, stirring occasionally.
3. Transfer the chicken and vegetables to a stockpot. Discard any fat left in the roasting pan. Add 1 cup of the water to the pan and deglaze over high heat, scraping up any browned bits sticking to the bottom of the pan.
4. Pour the liquid into the stockpot. Add the remaining ingredients and bring to a simmer. Skim the surface of the stock to remove any fat and foam, then gently simmer for 2½ hours.
5. Remove the stock from the heat and strain through cheesecloth or a fine mesh strainer. Let cool at room temperature. If the stock will not be used immediately, cover and refrigerate or freeze.

BEEF STOCK

Makes about 8 cups

This stock will provide more flavor than any store-bought beef stock. It will keep for 2 to 3 days in the refrigerator or up to 2 months in the freezer. Shank bones and marrow bones make a rich and flavorful stock. They are inexpensive and may be found in the meat section in most good supermarkets. For an even more intensely flavored stock, slowly simmer the strained stock until its volume is reduced by half.

2 tablespoons vegetable oil
6 pounds beef bones, chopped into
  2-inch pieces
1 onion, chopped
1 carrot, chopped
1 stalk celery, chopped
2 tablespoons chopped mushrooms

1 tomato, peeled, seeded,
  and chopped
3 cloves garlic, peeled
2 gallons cold water
1 bay leaf
2 sprigs fresh thyme
3 sprigs fresh parsley

1. Preheat the oven to 400°.
2. Cover the bottom of a roasting pan with the vegetable oil. Add the bones and vegetables; stir to coat with the oil. Roast until well browned, about 45 minutes, stirring occasionally.
3. Transfer the bones and vegetables to a stockpot. Discard the fat left in the roasting pan. Add 1 cup of the water to the pan and deglaze over high heat, scraping up any browned bits sticking to the bottom of the pan.
4. Pour the liquid into the stockpot. Add the remaining ingredients and bring to a simmer. Skim the surface to remove any fat and foam, then reduce the heat and gently simmer for 4 to 5 hours.
5. Remove the stock from the heat and strain through cheesecloth or a fine mesh strainer. Let cool at room temperature. If the stock will not be used immediately, cover and refrigerate or freeze.

VEGETABLE STOCK

Makes about 8 cups

This stock can be used as a base for soups and sauces, and in replacement of chicken or beef stock in vegetarian and low-fat dishes. For a darker, richer stock, sauté the vegetables longer, until they start to caramelize. Also, returning the strained stock to the heat and simmering until reduced by half will intensify the flavor. Dried mushrooms give the stock a more pronounced earthy flavor. If they are not available, fresh mushrooms can be substituted.

2 tablespoons butter	2 sprigs fresh thyme
1 onion, finely diced	2 bay leaves
1 leek, white part only, diced	1 teaspoon chopped fresh ginger
2 carrots, finely diced	1 teaspoon fennel seeds
2 stalks celery, finely diced	1 teaspoon salt
1 tomato, peeled, seeded, and diced	1 teaspoon whole black peppercorns
1 clove garlic, minced	12 cups cold water
3 sprigs fresh parsley	1 ounce dried shiitake mushrooms

1. Heat the butter in a stockpot over medium-high heat. Add the onion, leek, carrot, celery, tomato, and garlic; sauté for 4 to 5 minutes, stirring occasionally. Add the parsley, thyme, bay leaves, ginger, fennel, salt, peppercorns, and water. Bring to a boil; reduce the heat and slowly simmer the stock for 1 hour.
2. Remove the stock from the heat and pour through cheesecloth or a fine mesh strainer. Add the mushrooms and allow to steep for 30 minutes.
3. Strain the stock again and reserve the mushrooms for another use. Check the seasoning. Let the stock cool at room temperature. If it will not be used immediately, cover and refrigerate.

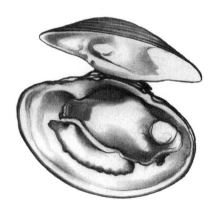

FISH STOCK

Makes about 8 cups

The key to good fish stock is clean, fresh fish bones. It is essential to thoroughly wash the bones and remove any organs or blood. Halibut, flounder, turbot, sole, and striped bass make excellent fish stock. Don't use oily fish such as mackerel, bluefish, salmon, or tuna. This stock will keep for 2 to 3 days in the refrigerator or 2 to 3 weeks in the freezer.

3 pounds fish bones
1 onion, chopped
2 carrots, chopped
1 stalk celery, chopped
2 cloves garlic, peeled
2 sprigs fresh parsley
2 sprigs fresh thyme

2 bay leaves
1 tablespoon chopped fresh fennel
1 tomato, peeled, seeded, and diced
1 cup dry white wine
1 slice lemon
10 cups cold water

1. Clean and rinse the fish bones under cold water; if using fish heads, remove the gills and any blood.
2. Place the bones in a large stockpot with the remaining ingredients. Bring to a slow simmer and cook for 30 minutes, skimming off any white foam as it rises to the surface.
3. Remove the stock from the heat and strain through cheesecloth or a fine mesh strainer. Let cool at room temperature. If the stock will not be used immediately, cover and refrigerate or freeze.

COURT BOUILLON

Makes about 4 cups

This makes an aromatic broth for poaching fish, shellfish, or chicken. It will keep for 2 to 3 days in the refrigerator.

4 cups water
1 cup dry white wine
2 small onions, diced
1 stalk celery, diced
1 carrot, diced
1 clove garlic, peeled
1 bay leaf

2 sprigs fresh parsley
1 tablespoon chopped fresh chives
2 sprigs fresh thyme
1 teaspoon salt
1 tablespoon black peppercorns
1 slice lemon

1. Combine all the ingredients in a large saucepan. Bring to a boil, then reduce the heat and gently simmer for 30 minutes.
2. Remove the pan from the heat and strain the liquid through cheesecloth or a fine mesh strainer. Discard the vegetables. Let the court bouillon cool at room temperature. If it will not be used immediately, cover and refrigerate.

LOBSTER STOCK

Lobster stock is a valuable contribution to many soups and sauces served with fish. This stock tastes best when used the same day it is made. However, if necessary, it will keep for 1 to 2 days in the refrigerator or up to 1 month in the freezer.

2 lobsters (1½ pounds each)	1 sprig fresh thyme
2 tablespoons olive oil	1 tablespoon chopped fresh chervil
1 onion, finely diced	1 bay leaf
1 carrot, finely diced	1 cup dry white wine
1 stalk celery, finely diced	7 cups cold water
1 clove garlic, finely diced	1 tablespoon lemon juice
2 tablespoons chopped fresh parsley	

1. Steam or boil the lobsters for 10 minutes. Remove from heat and allow to cool.
2. Remove the lobster meat from the tail and claw sections and reserve for another use. Split the body section of the lobster in half and discard the green tomalley, the sand sac behind the eyes, and the gill tissues. Rinse the body section under cold water. Chop the body and the tail and claw shells into small pieces for the stock.
3. Heat the olive oil in a stockpot over medium heat. Add the onion, carrot, celery, and garlic. Cook until lightly browned, 8 to 10 minutes, stirring occasionally. Add the chopped lobster shells along with the remaining ingredients. Bring to a simmer. Skim the surface of the stock to remove any fat and foam, then gently simmer for 30 minutes.
4. Remove the stock from the heat and strain through cheesecloth or a fine mesh strainer. Let cool at room temperature. If the stock will not be used immediately, cover and refrigerate or freeze.

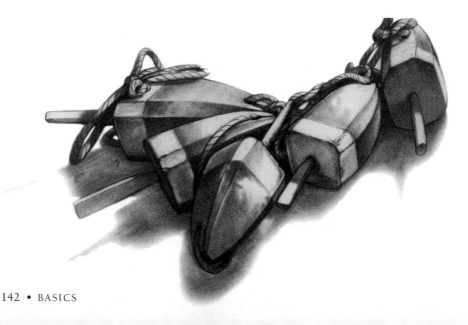

BASIC PASTA DOUGH

Makes about 1 pound

Always use good-quality flour when making pasta. Semolina flour is made from durum wheat, which is hard and high in gluten. It is not as finely ground as white flours but has a more coarsely ground texture. Gluten is a protein in flour that gives elasticity and structure to dough. Because semolina flour has a high gluten content, it produces a strong, fast-drying pasta most fitting for pasta dishes requiring heavy sauces. Pasta made with all-purpose flour, which is a blend of hard and soft wheat, produces a soft and lighter dough with a finer texture most suitable for ravioli and dishes that require delicate sauces.

1 cup unbleached all-purpose
   flour or as needed

1 cup semolina flour
1 teaspoon salt

1. Mix the flours and salt in a bowl and make a well in the center. Add the eggs, oil, and water to the well. With a fork, beat together the eggs, oil, and water, then begin to slowly incorporate the flour until the mixture starts to come together and forms a sticky mass of dough. With your hands press the dough into a ball. (If using a food processor, combine all the ingredients in the processor and process until dough forms, adding more water or flour if the dough is too dry or moist.)
2. Transfer the dough to a floured worktable and knead until smooth and elastic, about 10 minutes. The dough may need more flour or water while kneading, depending on its moisture content. Wrap the dough in a kitchen towel or plastic wrap and let stand for 1 hour at room temperature before rolling and cutting it.

PESTO

Makes about 1 cup

Reminiscent of summer, this versatile sauce works well with pizza, pasta, chicken, seafood, vegetables, and risotto. It will keep for 5 to 6 days in the refrigerator or up to 2 months in the freezer. Leave out the cheese if the pesto is to be frozen.

2 cups tightly packed fresh
   basil leaves, chopped
¼ cup tightly packed fresh
   parsley, chopped
2 cloves garlic, minced

¼ cup pine nuts, toasted
1 teaspoon lemon juice
½ cup olive oil
Salt and pepper
¼ cup grated Parmesan cheese

Place the basil, parsley, garlic, pine nuts, lemon juice, and olive oil in a blender or food processor; purée until smooth. Season with salt and pepper, then stir in the cheese. If the pesto will not be used immediately, cover and refrigerate.

PIZZA DOUGH

Makes two 10-inch pizza crusts

You can shape this dough into rounds, squares, or rectangles. An irregularly shaped pizza with a thick crust has a pleasing, rustic appearance. The thinner you press out the dough, the crisper the pizza will be. A thicker dough will produce a hard crust and a soft interior. When selecting a topping for pizza, always use the freshest ingredients and your imagination. Experiment and create with different combinations of vegetables, herbs, cheeses, meats, and seafood.

1½ cups lukewarm water
  (about 110°)
1 tablespoon active dry yeast
Pinch of sugar

3 eggs, beaten
1 tablespoon olive oil
1 tablespoon water or as needed

1. Stir together the warm water, yeast, and sugar in a small bowl. Allow to proof for 10 minutes.
2. Place 2 cups of the flour in a large bowl and make a well in the center. Place the yeast mixture, salt, and oil in the well. Slowly work in the flour with your fingertips or a wooden spoon, adding more of the flour while mixing until the dough starts to come together.
3. Transfer the dough to a floured worktable and knead until smooth and elastic, about 10 minutes, adding more flour when necessary to prevent sticking. Place the dough in an oiled bowl, cover with a kitchen towel or plastic wrap, and let rise in a warm place (80° to 90°) until double in size, about 2 hours.
4. Punch down the dough and let rise, covered, for 20 minutes. Use the dough in a pizza of your choice.

SOURDOUGH STARTER

Makes about 3 cups

Sourdough starter gives bread a strong, somewhat tangy flavor, a chewy texture, and an uneven, rustic appearance. The goal in preparing a sourdough starter is to provide conditions that encourage the growth of wild yeast microorganisms: consistent temperature and the right amount of flour and water. Wild yeast are airborne, living all around us, and they feed on the potato and the water in which it was cooked. They live in the starter, and they give rise and flavor to the bread. Occasional refreshing of the starter will help the wild yeast to flourish.

1 russet potato	3 to 4 cups all-purpose flour
About 2¼ cups water	1 teaspoon salt
2½ cups organic bread flour	1 tablespoon olive oil

1. Peel the potato and cut into ½-inch pieces. Place in a small saucepan and cover with the water. Cook until the potato is soft, about 15 to 20 minutes.
2. Place the potato and the cooking liquid in a bowl and mash with a potato masher or a fork. Let cool to room temperature.
3. Stir in 2 cups of the flour and thoroughly mix together. Cover with plastic wrap and a kitchen towel and let stand at room temperature (about 70°) for 24 hours.
4. Stir the mixture with a spoon, then cover and let stand at room temperature for another 24 hours.
5. At this point the starter should be slightly gray in color and have small bubbles on the surface. Stir the starter, then cover and let stand at room temperature for 24 hours longer.
6. By this time the starter should have a mild sour smell. Stir in the remaining ¼ cup flour and ¼ cup tap water. Cover and let stand for 6 hours at room temperature.
7. Transfer the starter to a glass jar (a canning jar works well) and refrigerate until needed. If the starter will not be used weekly, refresh it with 2 tablespoons each bread flour and water every 4 to 5 days.

INDEX

THANKS TO ALL OUR CREW, ESPECIALLY:

*Vicki Hull, our manager, who
keeps the ship on course . . .*

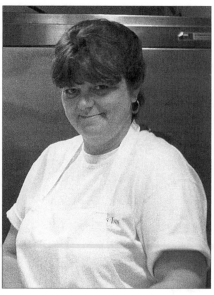

*to Elaine Webb, the assistant chef
who is Terry's first mate . . .*

*and to (from left to right) Rhonda Mitchell, Rhonda Eaton, Sandy Richter,
Jenn and Melissa Turner—some of the deck hands in the dining room.*

To order additional copies of *The Pilgrim's Inn Cookbook* send a check for $14.95 (per copy) plus $2 ($1 each additional copy) made payable to:

Pilgrim's Inn
P.O. Box 69
Deer Isle, ME 04627
or
Call 207-348-6615 • Fax 207-348-7769
with your VISA or MasterCard number.

For a Pilgrim's Inn brochure or reservations, use the information above.